THE BOOK OF Jeremiah

A Verse-By-Verse Bible Study
by

BETTE NORDBERG

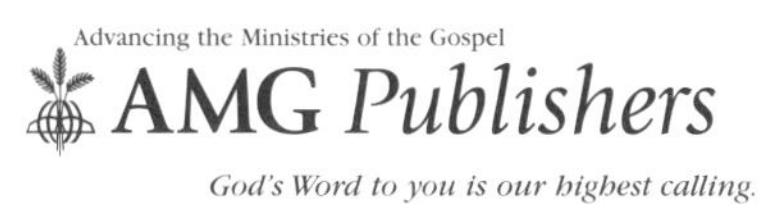

CHATTANOOGA, TENNESSEE

THE BOOK OF JEREMIAH

First Printing, 2008

ISBN 13: 978-089957-030-3

Cover design by Michael Largent
at Indoor Graphics, Chattanooga, TN (http://www.indoorgraphics.com/)

Editing and layout by Rick Steele at AMG Publishers

Printed in Canada
13 12 11 10 09 08 –T– 6 5 4 3 2 1

This book is dedicated to:

The Thursday Morning Ladies

Your love helped me finish!

And to Dan,

You've lived with the Kingdom ever in mind

About the Author

In 1977, Bette Nordberg graduated with a BS in Physical Therapy from the University of Washington. Since 1990, she has been published in periodicals, in drama venues, devotions, and books—both fiction and non-fiction. Her fiction projects include the award-winning *Serenity Bay* (Bethany House Publishers, 2000) and *Thin Air* (Bethany House, 2002). Non Fiction projects include *Encouraging Words for the First Hundred Days* (AMG Publishers, 2003).

Bette and her husband Kim (married 32 years) have four children, two college graduates and two WSU students. They make their home in Puyallup, Washington, where they helped plant Lighthouse Christian Church. At church, Bette edits the women's ministry newsletter and teaches Christian Life Classes. In her free time, Bette plays cello, knits and rides her well-worn Trek 5200 bicycle.

You may visit her website at:

www.bettenordberg.com

About the Following God Series

Three authors and fellow ministers, Wayne Barber, Eddie Rasnake, and Rick Shepherd, teamed up in 1998 to write a character-based Bible study for AMG Publishers. Their collaboration developed into the title, *Life Principles from the Old Testament.* Since 1998 these same authors and AMG Publishers have produced five more character-based studies—each consisting of twelve lessons geared around a five-day study of a particular Bible personality. More studies of this type are in the works. In 2003, AMG Publishers began publishing Following God workbooks that served as verse-by-verse studies of certain books of the Bible. This release of *The Book of Jeremiah* becomes the third title of this type released in the Following God™ **Through the Bible Series.** Though new studies and authors are being introduced, the interactive study format that readers have come to love remains constant with each new Following God™ release. As new titles and categories are being planned, our focus remains the same: to provide excellent Bible study materials that point people to God's Word in ways that allow them to apply truths to their own lives. More information on this groundbreaking series can be found on the following web page:

www.amgpublishers.com

Table of Contents

The Book of Jeremiah

INTRODUCTION

Jeremiah? Are you kidding? Why would anyone want to study Jeremiah? After all, it's such a depressing book! What could possibly be relevant about a book written more than 2,500 years ago?

If you wonder about the value of Jeremiah, you're not alone.

Most Bible students find plenty to challenge them on the pages of the New Testament. "Let's focus on something encouraging," they insist, "something relevant. After all, what do we have in common with those Old Testament guys, anyway?"

I used to ask myself the same question.

Truthfully? People aren't all that different—no matter when they live. The folks listening to Jeremiah nearly three thousand years ago struggled with many of the same issues we do. They had trouble keeping their priorities straight. They fought with unbelief. They were proud, reluctant to admit that they had flaws, or made real mistakes. They wanted to see themselves in the best light, even if that meant missing out on God's honest evaluation of their situation.

The folks listening to Jeremiah nearly three thousand years ago struggled with many of the same issues we do. They had trouble keeping their priorities straight. They fought with unbelief. They were proud, reluctant to admit that they had flaws or made real mistakes.

Jeremiah's words are as relevant today as they were to the citizens of Jerusalem seven hundred years before Jesus' birth. Like many Old Testament books, willing students have discovered in Jeremiah some of the most encouraging truths in the entire Old Testament.

Of course, all biblical truth comes from God. In Jeremiah you'll discover these truths are revealed by different voices. As you study this complex book, you'll learn to identify exactly who is speaking. You'll be able to differentiate between Jeremiah's voice and God's. You'll learn to identify God's messages through Jeremiah to the people, God's personal words of encouragement to Jeremiah, His servant, and God's commentary about His own feelings and relationship with the people of Judah, Babylon, and the surrounding nations.

When the words in Jeremiah are spoken by God, you'll recognize them by their quotation marks and the accompanying attribution. Other memorable verses are the words of Jeremiah himself, who, while facing incredibly difficult circumstances, determined that he would honor God with his words, with his actions, and with his attitude.

In light of Jeremiah's commitment and persistence, you'll discover that this prophet was a biblical hero of epic proportions.

We might compare Jeremiah to a modern Hudson Taylor, Billy Graham, or Oswald Chambers. For most of his adult life, Jeremiah worked full-time to convince the nation of Judah to repent.

We might compare him to a modern Hudson Taylor, Billy Graham, or Oswald Chambers. For most of his adult life, Jeremiah worked full-time to convince the nation of Judah to repent. As a speaker, a writer, a leader, and a confidant of the king, most would agree that Jeremiah continued to serve God wholeheartedly despite widespread rejection of his message. Now that takes a hero's courage!

While Jeremiah was a hero, he was also undoubtedly human.

Even as he served, he struggled with questions—questions about his own purpose, about the effectiveness of his work, about God's sovereignty, and about the fate of his people. He fought with emotions so strong that they occasionally overwhelmed his willingness to live. The book bearing his name gives ample evidence of both sides—hero and human—of this extraordinary man.

Though this godly man inspires me, inspiration is not all I find in the book of Jeremiah.

From these pages, we learn about Jeremiah's time, his culture, and his people. We come to understand the people's prevailing attitude toward God, the fear surrounding their everyday lives, and the struggles of Judah in an era of international instability.

And, we can learn much about the God we serve. A careful reading of Jeremiah is enough to craft an incredibly accurate characterization of God. On these pages, God reveals His power, His plan for His people, His passion, and His concern for those He loves. As we study, we learn much about God's intentions, His methods, and His discipline.

Jeremiah lived in a dark era, a time when everyone around him had grown tired of the religious traditions and requirements of their forefathers. The people of Judah were fed up and worn out. They'd decided to go their own way, throwing out the rules and morals of their ancestors. Desperate, they'd decided to try anything, any god or religion, any tradition that might keep them out of the hands of their enemies. These people would do almost anything to avoid the political forces that threatened their very existence.

How far had the people fallen? When Jeremiah first started preaching, Josiah reigned as king over Judah. In those days, people worshiped Baal and Asherah inside the Lord's temple. They sacrificed their own children to Molech in the valley of Ben-hinnom. Altars to foreign gods had been erected both in the temple and on the roof of the king's palace. Throughout the land mediums, psychics, pagan priests and household gods were everywhere. There were pagan shrines at the gates of Jerusalem, on the city streets, and even in the courtyard of the Lord's temple. The nation of Judah had turned away from faith in the one true God, and had chosen to worship multiple gods, exactly as the pagan nations around them.

Though our culture does not face the immediate threat of invasion and annihilation by another nation, people today are very similar to the Judeans of Jeremiah's time. In our generation, people have thrown out much of their Judeo-Christian heritage.

I live in Washington State where we boast one of the lowest rates of church-attendance in the USA. Like the people in Jeremiah's world, many of us, Christians included, have gone our own way. We believe in relative values. We make our own rules. We resist authority. We despise the group-thinking imposed by "religion," instead cherishing our independence above nearly every other value. We value independent thinking and individual rights more than group morality. Many in our culture foolishly believe that any faith is equally valid, provided that it is sincerely followed.

Our culture makes Jeremiah's audience seem pretty contemporary, doesn't it?

As we study this book, we'll see how similar our world is to the one Jeremiah faced. Like him, we live in a culture where the religious traditions and beliefs of our forefathers are mocked and rejected. Our society, like his, is frequently motivated by fear—fear of terrorists, fear of poverty, fear of loneliness, and the fear of consequences. To be completely truthful, even Christian believers often wonder, as Jeremiah did, what God intends to accomplish in our time.

To be truthful, we often wonder, as Jeremiah did, what God intends to accomplish in our time.

In this light, the book of Jeremiah is surprisingly current.

Like Jeremiah, we long to make a difference, but fear we may not. We yearn to change our world, but watch helplessly as parts of the church, and the nation around us continue to make decisions that grieve the heart of God. We find ourselves weary and discouraged. Some of us even fight despair.

How can we persevere? In the face of this disintegrating culture, how can we maintain the joy we know in Christ? How can we trust God when all around us, we watch believers and non-believers alike reject God's kingdom principles?

It isn't easy. But somehow, we must learn to keep our eyes on God. We must cling to His principles and truths. We must find a way to believe even when all around us turn away.

Looking into the book of Jeremiah, we find this kind of hope. We'll see God work both in and through His servant. We'll come to trust God's sovereign plan for the church and for us as ministers. We'll learn to see his hand in the details of His provision—even in the most challenging of circumstances. As happens every time we look deeply into the Word of God, we'll be changed! I guarantee it.

Organizing your study:
I highly recommend that you work through this study in a group; you'll benefit from the insights and applications your fellow students share. Perhaps you can persuade one of your peers to lead you through the entire eight sessions. Even without a formal teacher, I've even seen groups successfully take turns leading weekly discussions—each leader choosing to emphasize the questions he/she feels are most important.

Over the course of our study, we won't cover every verse in Jeremiah, or even every chapter. Instead, we'll focus on the major themes of the book, pausing long enough to recognize and apply the principles therein. Hopefully, during our eight weeks together, you'll find time to read the entire book as well as finish the weekly studies.

The weekly lessons include questions grouped in five daily sections. Tackle this workload with whatever approach works for you. You may choose to answer only one section each day, pacing yourself throughout the week according to the demands of your schedule. Or, you may choose to do all your work in one sitting. When I had four very young children, I did my homework the night before my Bible study met. Otherwise, I knew I'd forget everything I'd learned!

If you're feeling a little insecure, perhaps you could meet a more experienced friend for coffee and answer the questions together. You might even want to finish the questions the week *after* the presentations of your group leader. If you do this, I suspect you'll miss the joy of discovering biblical truth under your own steam. On the other hand, by doing the questions later you'll have at least one advantage: you'll already know what you're looking for, and you may find that you are better able to remember the truths you discover.

Do whatever works for you.
Each of us must learn to work with the Word of God in our own way. As we explore the scriptures, we'll find ourselves growing in knowledge, in wisdom and in faith. I make these promises without hesitation.

Begin each study session with a simple prayer: Invite the Holy Spirit to help you as you study. Thank Him for granting you the privilege of studying His word, for the freedom to study openly, and for the resources to do so. Thank Him ahead of time for the truth He will teach you. He is pleased to guide you as you dig into His Word.

What can you expect from this workbook?
In each of our eight studies, we'll focus on three major themes. As you read through the text and mark your Bible, you might consider color-coding your markings. Choose a different color pencil or highlighter for each of the following topics:

First, we'll learn about the person of Jeremiah.
Who was this Old Testament giant? What was he like? What kind of faith did he have? What sustained him through more than forty-six years of ministry? As we answer these questions we'll pause and reflect on our own ministry and compare our responses with Jeremiah's. We'll ask ourselves how we measure up to this faithful prophet. Before we finish, we'll let God use this portrait to encourage us to greater faithfulness and service.

Second, we'll focus on the people of God.
Of course the Book of Jeremiah doesn't talk about Christians. Jeremiah's words were originally directed to Old Testament believers—men and women committed to God via the Old Covenant. Though this concept may be new to you, you'll understand this more clearly over the course of our study. We'll consider the choices they made and what happened as a result of those choices. We'll look at how these people responded to God. And, we'll ask ourselves if we are like these believing, but disobedient people.

Most importantly, we'll learn about God.
As we dig through the book of Jeremiah, we'll consider these kinds of questions:

If God had a list of pet peeves, what would be on the list?

What really makes Him angry?

How does God respond to rebellion?

What do you know about His heart?

What is His first wish for His people?

How does God respond to repentance?

As we look at God's words and actions in the Book of Jeremiah, we'll come to know God more intimately. We'll begin to understand His deepest feelings and learn more about the things that make Him angry. We'll know what He wishes for. We'll understand what He hopes to accomplish when He designs our correction.

How will this study change you?
Perhaps you remember a particular sermon where you thought to yourself, *I wish I could understand scripture like that. I just can't seem to dig those ideas out on my own.*

The truth is, with practice, all believers—not just pastors and teachers—can learn to handle the scriptures accurately. Over the course of our time together, you'll begin to acquire tools to help you deepen your study of God's Word. Because all scriptures must be examined in light of the whole Bible, we'll make comparisons between verses in both the New and Old Testaments. We'll see how frequently the scriptures parallel one another, even though some of these passages were written nearly eight hundred years apart. As we do this, we'll avoid interpretation errors and faulty applications of the Jeremiah passages.

The truth is, with practice, all believers—not just pastors and teachers—can learn to handle the scriptures accurately.

I think you'll be unbelievably blessed by what you gather from the book of Jeremiah. What a rich experience we have before us!

A word about context
I've been reading the Bible for years now, and I've had the privilege of studying with some very gifted teachers. Still, over my years in the Word, I've watched many Bible students make one common mistake:

When reading the Old Testament, they fail to keep the context of the passage in mind.

What is context? In biblical studies, context refers to the words, phrases and passages surrounding the biblical text under examination. Let me give you some simple examples.

In your Bible, the four chapters of John 14 through 17 probably appear in red ink. This is because modern Bibles print the words of Jesus in red. These important chapters have a context. They are the words that Jesus shares with His closest companions—His disciples—only hours before His arrest, trial, and crucifixion. They are the last instructions He shares with them before His death. The context, or environment surrounding these words, helps us to recognize how important these thoughts were to Jesus.

If it helps, think about your last days on earth. If you knew that you were about to die, wouldn't you gather those you love and give them last instructions or encouragement? Wouldn't you want to impart some wisdom to help them persevere in their faith? The context of these chapters in John, these last words of Jesus, implies that these are the most important things Jesus wanted His disciples to remember.

Here's another example. The book of Thessalonians was written in the context of a question that perplexed the church at Thessalonica. They believed in the imminent return of Christ, but worried about what might happen to those who died before Christ returned. The context of the book then, is Paul's clarification of this question for his readers—to reassure them concerning those who had already died. This background explains the presence of passages in chapters 4 and 5 that are so frequently quoted in modern churches.

The people in Jeremiah's audience had a unique and specific relationship with God. We call it a covenant relationship.

The Book of Jeremiah has context too!

The people in Jeremiah's audience had a unique and specific relationship with God. We call it a covenant relationship. You can read about the beginning of this covenant relationship in the book of Genesis, chapter 17. Here Abram, who later is renamed Abraham, the father of the nation of Israel, enters into a unique relationship with God. This everlasting relationship, initiated by God, involves the commitment of both parties. For his part, Abram promises to love and serve God wholeheartedly. In return, God promises to be Abraham's God and to bless Abraham with descendants as numerous as the stars.

The sign of this covenant relationship is the ceremonial practice of circumcision. Each male born into Abram's family was to be circumcised on the eighth day after his birth. You'll find more information about circumcision in the lessons that follow.

Interestingly, by the time the Book of Jeremiah opens, the Jewish people have had many opportunities to renew this covenant with God. They did so after Moses presented them with the Ten Commandments. They did so again when they entered the Promised Land—the land of Israel. King Josiah encouraged the people to renew this covenant during his reign. Occasionally throughout Israel's history, a godly leader would arise and lead the people through a renewal of the covenant.

The context, then, of Jeremiah's book, is one of covenant relationship (an irrevocably committed relationship between God and the Jewish people). The people of Jeremiah's audience had recently recommitted to their covenant relationship with God. They knew who God is. They knew what He expected. They had committed to keeping His laws and statutes and ordinances. In fact, the most recent renewal of their covenant relationship occurs under King Josiah, just a few years before Jeremiah begins his ministry.

For this reason, we cannot accurately compare Jeremiah's audience with our contemporary culture. The people of the United States (as a nation) have never entered into a binding covenant relationship with God (nor has any other modern nation, for that matter). Today, covenant relationships exist only between **individuals** and God.

Our covenant relationship with God is a **new** covenant relationship. It is not based on rules and regulations, nor is it dependent on daily sacrifices or rituals. It is based on the unearned gift of eternal life, offered to us by God the

Father, and purchased for us by Jesus' death on the cross. We have relationship with God based **solely** on Jesus' sacrifice. He died once for all. And that was enough.

Keep these ideas in mind as you attempt to apply the lessons you learn in the book of Jeremiah. Be careful not to assume that God's corrections belong only to the unbelieving world around you. Though the people in our culture have certainly abandoned godly values, God does not expect of our nation what He expected of Jeremiah's audience.

This is not to say that he approves of our nation's immorality or the rampant evil throughout our world for that matter. Not at all. But, God has a very different standard for His children. In truth, God's standards are much higher.

As you apply the Jeremiah lessons, think first about yourself, and then about the church. We exist in a new covenant relationship with God. Our new covenant relationship with God makes Jeremiah's sermons incredibly applicable to us.

Our new covenant relationship with God makes Jeremiah's sermons incredibly applicable to us.

Don't be afraid to ask yourself difficult questions. How have I abandoned God? How have I turned to other gods (figuratively speaking) to solve my problems? How have I sacrificed my children in order to pursue the things I value? As you consider these issues, ask the Holy Spirit to show you which applications require your attention. Respond to Him. Rejoice in His revelation. God has much to share with you in the days ahead!

An overview of the Bible

Many students have a difficult time understanding the "big picture" when they look at the Old Testament. The various Old Testament books (39 in all) seem to have little to do with one another. The people involved, the cultures they reflect, the timeline of the books seem obscure and difficult to follow.

If you took an ordinary piece of notebook paper and turned it sideways (in what your computer calls landscape mode), you might draw a line across the page depicting Old Testament biblical history. At the left end, you would write, "God creates man." This point would represent the beginning of the book of Genesis.

At the far right end of your line, you would write, "The church era begins." To the right, beyond the point where your paper ends, if the line continued it would represent the four Gospels, the book of Acts, and all of the New Testament Epistles, along with the book of Revelation.

The line on your paper, the one between Genesis and the Church Era accounts for roughly four thousand years of biblical history. I've attached a timeline chart for this time period on page 9. This timeline chart not only indicates significant eras in Israel's history, it also lists the books of the Old Testament in the approximate order they were written. (The Old Testament books are shown in italic type.)

The first eleven chapters of Genesis, (from creation to the beginning of Abraham's relationship with God) cover roughly two thousand years. Then suddenly, the biblical account slows and amplifies. The rest of Genesis covers the story of Abraham and his family all the way to Joseph and his brothers' travel to Egypt. This reflects only about three hundred years.

In its simplest form, the entire Old Testament is nothing more than the story of a family. Genesis, Exodus, Leviticus, Numbers, Deuteronomy and Joshua all follow the story of God choosing one man (Abraham) as His own possession. God and Abraham enter into an everlasting covenant. After leading Abraham to the Promised Land, God gives him a family.

Generations later, famine drives Abraham's grandchildren and great-grandchildren to Egypt. Over time, their hosts (the Egyptians) become their enemies, enslaving the Jewish people. Eventually, God uses Moses to lead this chosen group—now numbering over a million people—from Egypt to the Promised Land.

Abraham's descendants entered the Promised Land in roughly 1400 BC. There, the twelve tribes of this family establish themselves as a nation. But these people have trouble obeying God. The book of Judges (next on your time-line) tells story after story of their disobedience. Eventually, the Israelites beg God for a king, and He grants their desire. The year is roughly 1000 BC.

Next to Judges belong 1 and 2 Samuel, 1 and 2 Kings, and 1 and 2 Chronicles. These books tell the successive stories of the kings who ruled over God's people.

Now, observe in our timeline chart on the next page, around 1000 BC, the words **"Divided Kingdom."** You can read about the division of the nation in 1 Kings 12. Here ten tribes become the nation of Israel (the Northern Kingdom) and the tribes of Judah and Benjamin become the Southern Kingdom, also called the nation of Judah. (You will read about this in more detail later in this study). A detailed **Timeline of the Kings** chart is offered on page 145 that covers this era of divided kingdoms, and on page 143, the reigns of all the kings of both Israel and Judah are listed in order. Also, there is an excellent map of the divided kingdoms on page 141.

However God's family is divided for a short time. Not long after the separation of the two nations, Israel (the Northern Kingdom) is conquered by Assyria. In 722 BC, Assyria deports most of the Northern Kingdom's inhabitants from the land and replaces them with Assyrians.

The nation of Judah continues to exist for nearly 150 years before the Babylonians finally destroy Jerusalem in 586 BC. Then, after a series of attacks and deportations, King Nebuchadnezzar removes the inhabitants of Judah, leaving the land nearly empty. Seventy years later, the first of these captives begins to return to Israel. The people of Judah rebuild a provincial state that continues under the dominion of other empires through the next five centuries until the birth of Christ. During this time, several of the Minor Prophet Old Testament books are written, including Haggai, Zechariah, and Malachi.

Between the last of the Minor Prophets and Jesus' birth, we have a silent period of perhaps four hundred years, when there is no record of God speaking to his people.

Whenever you read the word "Israel," you need to ask yourself, "Does this passage refer to the person, the entire nation, the land itself, or the Northern Kingdom?

One more detail: in the Old Testament, the word, "Israel" can have at least four different meanings. It can refer to a person, Abraham's grandson, Jacob, who was renamed Israel after a particularly intense experience with the Angel of the Lord (see Genesis 32). The word can also refer to all of Jacob's descendants—the unified nation of Israel. Later, after the twelve tribes split into two nations, the Bible refers to the Northern Kingdom, with its capital in Samaria, as Israel. Today, the word also refers to the political

Creation (Origins of God's Family)	Family Develops Through Abraham	God's Family Becomes a Nation	Monarchy Begins with King Saul	Tribal Division under Divided Kingdoms	Submission to Foreign Nations

The Story of a Family: An Old Testament Timeline

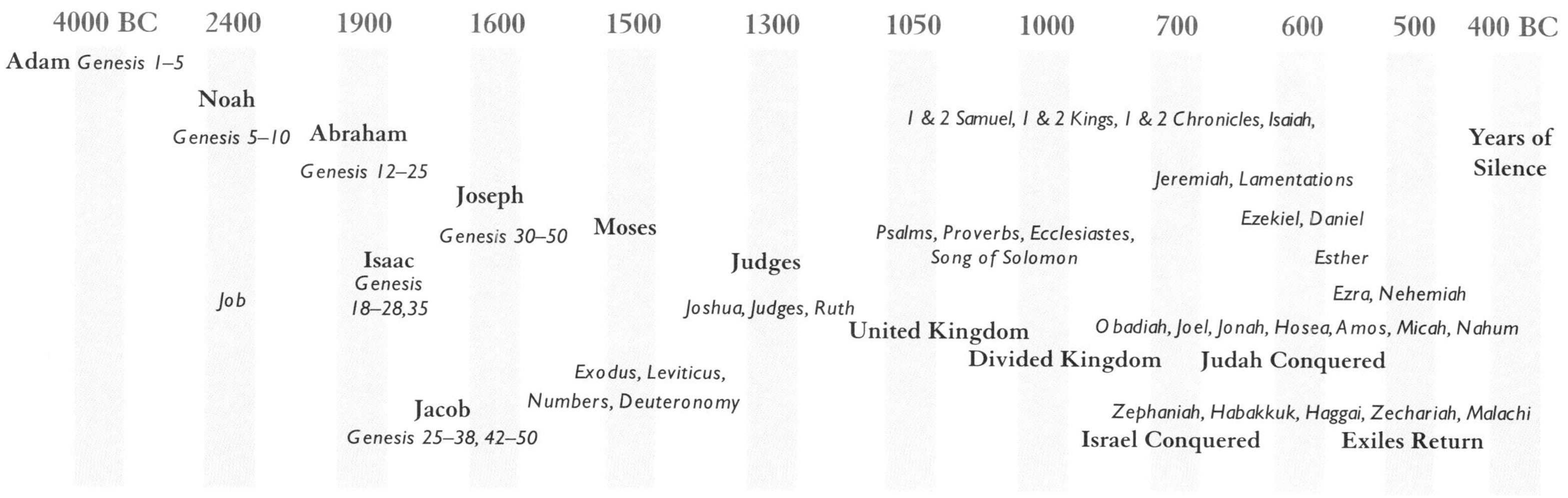

4000 BC · 2400 · 1900 · 1600 · 1500 · 1300 · 1050 · 1000 · 700 · 600 · 500 · 400 BC

Adam *Genesis 1–5*

Noah *Genesis 5–10*

Job

Abraham *Genesis 12–25*

Isaac *Genesis 18–28,35*

Jacob *Genesis 25–38, 42–50*

Joseph *Genesis 30–50*

Moses

Exodus, Leviticus, Numbers, Deuteronomy

Judges

Joshua, Judges, Ruth

1 & 2 Samuel, 1 & 2 Kings, 1 & 2 Chronicles, Isaiah,

Psalms, Proverbs, Ecclesiastes, Song of Solomon

United Kingdom

Divided Kingdom

Jeremiah, Lamentations

Ezekiel, Daniel

Esther

Ezra, Nehemiah

Obadiah, Joel, Jonah, Hosea, Amos, Micah, Nahum

Judah Conquered

Zephaniah, Habakkuk, Haggai, Zechariah, Malachi

Israel Conquered

Exiles Return

Years of Silence

and geographic Middle Eastern nation now located on part of what was once called the Promised Land.

Whenever you read the word "Israel," ask yourself, *Does this passage refer to the person? To the entire nation? To the land itself? Or, does this refer to the Northern Kingdom?* These questions will help you to clarify the meaning of biblical passages.

A word about translations

Some teachers put great emphasis on the accuracy of the various Bible translations available to students. For this study, you needn't worry about which version you use. You won't be required to do any heavy word studies. Because I've referred to several translations as I formulated my questions, your answers should be quite consistent from version to version. So relax! Use the translation that suits you best.

For my part, in general, I'll be quoting from the New Living Translation. I love the clarity of thought and story found there. Contemporary readers have no trouble discerning the meaning of this text. Remember that Jeremiah is a biographical and historical book—not unlike a contemporary biography of a president. We will be able to derive the same principles and patterns from Jeremiah no matter which version you choose.

Now, at last, we come to the first lesson. Remember, as you mine the Word of God for truth, your reward is proportional to your effort. Plan to set aside time for your study. Apply yourself. Attend class regularly. Bathe in the rich truths of Scripture!

Let's begin!

lesson 1

Jeremiah 1

GOD CALLS A YOUNG MAN

Introduction: Jeremiah's World:

In 1990, I began writing my first published project. *Evangeline, a Woman of Faith* took nearly six years to write. I wanted my audience to understand much more about Evangeline McNeill than simply how she founded and directed the Cannon Beach Christian Conference Center. I wanted them to know what kind of woman would defy the traditional definitions of women's ministry. I wanted readers to see her in action, to understand the power of her prayer life, to see her passion for evangelism, and sense her unusual ability to hear and obey God. It wasn't easy. By the time I began writing, Evangeline had been dead almost fifteen years. I had never met her.

Since I had no firsthand experience with Evangeline, I had to depend on the memories of those who knew and worked with her. Some had known Evangeline intimately; her sister and brother both granted hours of interviews. Others knew her only as a boss. Her daughter knew her as most daughters do; she was acutely aware of her mother's humanity and yet awed by the power and devotion of Evangeline's life. Beyond hours of interviews, I had some remaining physical evidence. Evangeline had saved every scrap of paper she accumulated over the course of her long life. I had menus, train tickets, notes from the backs of envelopes, grocery lists, and speech notes. Putting it all together was a little like piecing together a jigsaw puzzle without the box's front cover. I had most of the pieces; I just wasn't sure how they all fit.

"Get up and prepare for action. Go out and tell them everything I tell you to say. Do not be afraid of them, . . . For I am with you, and I will take care of you. I, the Lord, have spoken!"

Jeremiah 1:17–19

I won't know how accurate my work was until I meet Evangeline McNeill in heaven. The book of Jeremiah is very different. Here, Jeremiah tells us his own story. He includes his own feelings as he recounts the events of his life. Woven in with the narrative, you'll find intricate details about Jeremiah's background, his calling, his ministry, his relationship with God and the response of his audience. Unlike Evangeline's biography, written by a bystander many years after the fact, this book is written by the one who knew the story intimately—the main character. As you study, enjoy this up-close account of international intrigue, divine judgment, and personal anguish. Walk in Jeremiah's shoes. Feel his feelings. Sense his sorrow. Listen as he struggles to obey God in the face of his own self-doubt.

It is a story you won't soon forget.

In the book of Jeremiah, you'll find more personal information about the "weeping prophet" than the Bible reveals about any other Old Testament prophet. This biographical material requires careful observation of the text; but you'll be delighted by what you discover!

Unfortunately, the text doesn't explain much about the political and social environment where Jeremiah served his people. While some details can be found in other Old Testament passages, I'll provide additional historical background wherever we need it.

Jeremiah 1

DAY ONE

WHO WAS JEREMIAH

From the perspective of Middle Eastern history, the Promised Land has long been attractive to her neighbors. Along Israel's rich western plain, one of the region's primary trade routes ran roughly North-South along the Mediterranean Sea from Egypt to Turkey. Because this route ensured the passage of goods into and out of the region, they provided vital access to any goods not produced within the region itself. In addition, control of these roads provided the potential for additional tax revenue. From ancient days through the fall of the Roman Empire, nations have fought for control of these valuable Mediterranean trade routes.

For empires lying East of Palestine, the nation of Israel blocked access to the Mediterranean Sea. Since sea trade required protected seaports, nations wanting to develop this resource needed to control Israel. Thus, neighboring nations lusted over Israel's access to the sea, and nation after nation determined to conquer and occupy her valuable seacoast.

Plentiful rain and rich soil make Israel incredibly fertile. Empires eagerly fought over her agricultural potential. In Jeremiah's day, food and water were riches indeed.

Perhaps most importantly through commanding these roads, kingdoms controlled primary access routes opposing nations would use to bring in warring equipment and soldiers. These roads guaranteed national security.

However, from God's perspective, regional politics were not simply politics. Certainly, the Bible shows us God's deep concern for these foreign nations and their rulers. But God also used their greed and violence to discipline His people. Enemy empires and kings, rulers and generals were sometimes valuable tools in God's mighty hand. You will see this clearly revealed in Scripture as you continue your study journey.

Most scholars date the call of Jeremiah (the book's opening chapter) to 627 BC.

Remember, before Jeremiah began preaching, Israel had already divided herself into two separate nations, each with its own king and capital (see the Kings of Israel and Judah chart on p. 143). "Israel" referred to the northern portion of Palestine, and to ten of the original twelve tribes born to Jacob. "Judah" referred to the southern region surrounding Jerusalem, as well as to the land and cities given to the tribes of Judah and Benjamin.

Three empires played significant roles in the history surrounding the book of Jeremiah. They were Egypt, Assyria, and Babylon. During the last years of the Southern Kingdom's existence these three empires fought for dominance over the entire Middle East; in the process each fought for control of Israel. (In our final lesson, we'll look at how the Persian Empire divinely entered into the history of God's people.)

When the book of Jeremiah opens, conditions in the region were rapidly changing. For centuries the Assyrian Empire had dominated the region. So strong was her influence, that roughly one hundred years before the opening of Jeremiah, Assyria ended a three-year siege of Samaria (the Northern Kingdom's capital city) in 722 BC, by destroying the city and deporting her citizens (see 2 Kings 17:5).

Certainly, Jeremiah's audience understood the Assyrian threat. To them, the fall of Samaria was recent history—as recent to them as our Civil War is to us. Residents of Jerusalem had narrowly escaped their own siege by the Assyrian army (see 2 Kings 18—19).

When Jeremiah began his ministry, a new and more frightening empire threatens Judah. Jeremiah's audience was keenly aware of this danger. While Jeremiah preached, their kingdom stood on the brink of impending disaster.

Just one year after God called Jeremiah, in 626 BC, the Babylonian army conquered the Assyrians outside of Babylon. Their power was further strengthened when they defeated Nineveh (the Assyrian Capital) in 612 BC. The Babylonian army had managed to crush Assyrian dominion.

In 609 BC Egypt joined Assyria in one desperate effort to regain lost territory from Babylon. Judah recognized Egypt as its largest threat. Wanting to prevent Egypt's victory, Judah joined Assyria in its fight against Egypt on the plains of Megiddo. Unfortunately Egypt's Pharaoh Neco defeated Judah, and for a short time Egypt assumed control of Palestine. These are the events surrounding the opening of Jeremiah's ministry.

Though Babylon experienced a temporary setback, it would not be long before she fully defeated Egypt, ending its regional dominance. Then, with both Egypt and Assyria out of his way, Nebuchadnezzar (Babylon's leader) set his sights on Palestine,

While Jeremiah called Judah to repentance, the nation's newest enemy stood

Understanding the Old Testament can be a challenge, even for experienced Bible students. After all, when God delivers the Israelites from slavery, Moses leads **one** nation out of Egypt. But by the middle of I Kings, things have changed; the twelve tribes have become two separate and warring nations.

The explanation: After forty years of wandering, the twelve tribes (603,000 men) enter the Promised Land under Joshua. After Joshua's death, the era of Judges begins. This period of roughly four hundred years marks a slow but persistent decline in the spiritual commitment of God's people. Eventually, Saul is anointed as Israel's first king; the Jewish nation unites. Under King David, Israel develops national security. Under David's son, Solomon, the Temple is constructed. The nation does not remain united for long.

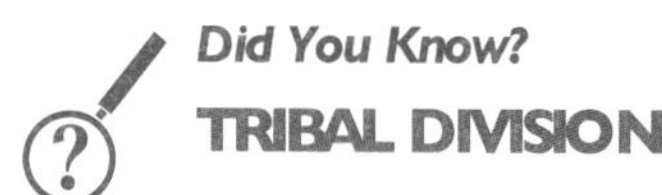

When Solomon died his son Rehoboam became king. Under his rule, the northern ten tribes revolted, naming Jereboam as their king and establishing Samaria as their capital. Only the tribes of Benjamin and Judah remained loyal to David's dynasty. From this point on, the book of Kings uses the term "Israel" to refer to the northern tribes, and "Judah" to refer to David's dynasty, centered in Jerusalem

outside the gates. If anything, this overshadowing threat should have sharpened the hearing of Judah's citizens. Imminent danger should have encouraged them to seek God. Perhaps they should have recognized God as their only deliverance. But as we shall see, danger seemed to have no effect on Jeremiah's audience. Instead, the people of Judah continued their folly.

Examining the Text:
Beginning in Jeremiah, use the first two verses to discover a bit about Jeremiah. What was his background? Where was he from?

Our background has a great deal to do with the person we become. As the son of a priest, Jeremiah probably had an entirely different upbringing than the son of a farmer, or a carpenter. God, through Moses, established the priesthood in the book of Exodus. You can read about the very first ordination in Exodus 28. In Exodus 28:1, God says, *"Your brother, Aaron, and his sons, Nadab Abihu, Eleazar, and Ithamar, will be set apart from the common people."*

"But you are a chosen people, a royal priesthood, a holy nation, a people belonging to God, that you may declare the praises of him <u>who called you</u> out of darkness into his wonderful light."

I Peter 2:9 (emphasis mine)

Beginning in 1 Chronicles 6:48, this duty is further clarified:

> *Their relatives, also Levites were appointed to various other tasks in the Tabernacle, the house of God. Only Aaron and his descendants served as priests. They presented the offering on the altar of burnt offering and the altar of incense, and they performed all the other duties related to the Most Holy Place. They made atonement for Israel by following all the commands that Moses, the servant of God had given them.*

📖 Look at Numbers 18:1–7, and define the difference between Priests and Levites.

How do you think Jeremiah's background might have influenced his growth as a person?

📖 Without using your footnotes, turn to 2 Kings and calculate how many years Jeremiah served in ministry. (You'll want to use the information in 2 Kings 22:1; 23:31; 23:36 and 24:8, 18.) In the space below, write down your calculations. For future reference you might also want to note in the margins of your Bible how long Jeremiah served.

Using these passages in 2 Kings, we can add the number of years each king served, from Josiah to Zedekiah, and account for at least forty years of continuous ministry. Later in Jeremiah, we'll discover that Jeremiah continued to serve beyond the eleventh year of Zedekiah. Tradition has it, that Jeremiah lived and ministered another six years in Egypt.

📖 In the space below, copy Jeremiah 1:3. Underline the event that signaled the end of Jeremiah's ministry. Keep this last phrase in mind as you read the messages Jeremiah shares with his people.

Most of us hope that our ministry ends with great success. Dwight Moody, a traveling shoe salesman, began holding Sunday school for street children in an abandoned Chicago saloon. By the time his life ended, his meager school had grown into one of Chicago's most prominent churches. At one point in 1897, the Chicago Avenue Church (seating 10,000) was filled to capacity with another six thousand people waiting outside.

Interestingly, God's plans for Jeremiah did not include this kind of success. In fact, though Jeremiah was called to bring the message of repentance to his people, his audience never really responded. In the end, Jeremiah's people suffered the consequence of their own disobedience. His messages seemed to echo in the canyons of rebelliousness and idolatry.

God's Plan for Jeremiah

Jeremiah 1

DAY TWO

At one point in his life, Jeremiah had a remarkable experience. In today's language, we might explain that experience by saying that God called him. In verse 5 note FOUR separate facts about God's relationship with Jeremiah before he was born.

1. ______
2. ______
3. ______
4. ______

📖 Now look at Psalm 139, which I've quoted here in the sidebar. Are God's statements about Jeremiah consistent with this passage? Do you think that this pre-birth action pertains only to Jeremiah?

Our modern culture stresses perfection, achievement, and success. Often, when I look in the mirror, all I notice are the flaws. Freckles. Wrinkles. Gray

PSALM 139:13–16

You made all the delicate, inner parts of my body and knit me together in my mother's womb. Thank you for making me so wonderfully complex! Your workmanship is marvelous—and how well I know it. You watched me as I was being formed in utter seclusion, as I was woven together in the dark of the womb. You saw me even before I was born. Every day of my life was recorded in your book. Every moment was laid out before a single day had passed.

hair. A square, muscular body. I stand in the mirror wishing for a model's skin, a Ballerina body, and "shampoo commercial" hair. When I look at my life, I often focus on the character flaws. Impatience. Quick temper. Pride.

I rarely reflect on who I am based on scriptural truths. If I would see myself as God sees me, I would see that every part of me has been created by God. I would recognize all of my days are part of His shaping plan for my character. I would begin to view failures as learning opportunities. Though I would recognize my own imperfection, I would also anticipate God's work in my character, knowing that I am not yet who I shall become.

From these scriptures (both Jeremiah and Psalms), what might you conclude about God's action in your own PRE-BIRTH life? Which of these four facts is the hardest for you to imagine or accept about your pre-birth relationship with God? Why do you think you might have trouble believing these facts?

Does every Christian have a calling? Refer to Romans 1:6 and 1 Peter 4:11 as you consider your answer.

Therefore, go and make disciples of all the nations, baptizing them in the name of the Father and the Son and the Holy Spirit. Teach these new disciples to obey all the commands I have given you. And be sure of this: I am with you always, even to the end of the age."

Matthew 28:19–20

First Peter 4:11 says, *"Are you called to be a speaker? Then speak as though God himself were speaking through you. Are you called to help others? Do it with all the strength and energy that God supplies. . . ."* Why do you think that a gift might be associated with a calling?

This idea of calling is not limited to the Old Testament. Contemporary believers have been called into a relationship with God through their new life in Christ. The Holy Spirit has given each of us at least one spiritual gift and called us to use our gifts for the good of the body of Christ. Perhaps we can broaden our definition of calling. Using all of these scriptures, it seems that a calling is an active work of the Holy Spirit in the life of God's children, whereby He molds us into a new level of responsibility and obedience. These incidents seem not to be once in a lifetime events, but rather the normal experience of one who trusts and believes in God.

📖 What was Jeremiah's response to God's formal "calling" (see 1:6)? In light of all God had already said to him, where was Jeremiah's focus?

Here is another way in which I am very much like Jeremiah. When I sense God asking me to complete a difficult task, my first response is often to make certain that God understands why I can't do it. *I'm too inexperienced,* I object. *I'm not well enough known. . . . I'm afraid. . . . People will hate it. . . . I can't sell it.*

No matter how we wrap our objections, our purpose is likely to get out of the calling. Jeremiah wanted to convince God that his age disqualified him from service. Jeremiah didn't focus on God's power or God's ability to work through a young man. Instead, Jeremiah looked only at himself, looking at his own flaws and lack of ability.

Like Jeremiah, I often respond to God based on my ability or lack thereof rather than focusing on His power and faithfulness. Sometimes, I wonder if I will ever learn.

Responding to the Call

Jeremiah 1

DAY THREE

How does the Lord respond to Jeremiah (1:7–8)?

____

____

Looking at verse 8, what emotion seemed to plague Jeremiah? Why do you think he felt this way? How does this same emotion manifest itself in you? How do your family members know when you are afraid?

____

____

____

When we are aware of our own fear cues, we can respond to our underlying emotions before they get the better of us. Perhaps you chew your fingernails when you're feeling anxious, or you get cranky with others. Perhaps you feel your heart beat rapidly, or your mouth get dry. I have a friend whose stomach cramps when she feels anxious. Once, when I was with an actress backstage, I asked her how she was feeling.

"I'm fine," she answered, her voice trembling and her face pale. "I have to go throw up, now. I'll be right back."

I tend to become short-tempered and loud. My daughter expresses anxiety the same way. Sometimes, I eat to ease my fears. One of my sons becomes very quiet, almost aloof. Knowing myself allows me to be aware of what is happening inside me, and choose trust over fear. This way I can let go of unproductive behavior—before it damages me, or someone I love.

It can be just as helpful to be aware of the fear cues in the people around me. When I know how this emotion affects those I love, I can help them work through their feelings without taking their behavior personally. It's not a bad idea to become an observer of your friends and family. See if you can track their emotions through the subtleties of their behavior.

📖 In Jeremiah 1:8 what was God's two-fold promise to Jeremiah? Do these words sound familiar to you? Where have you read similar words?

____

📖 Turn to the last few verses of Matthew's gospel (chapter 28). What does Jesus promise His followers? How does it feel to know that God will be with you as you serve Him? In what ways have you experienced the Lord's care for you in the last twenty-four hours? In the last forty-eight hours? In the last week?

____

____

____

One of the most prevalent phrases in the Old Testament, "I will be with you," can be found over and over as God calls His people to action. He used this exact phrase in speaking with Isaac, Jacob, Moses, Joshua, Gideon, and Solomon. Similar phrases are used in numerous other instances. You can use these scriptures to support the principle: When God calls His people to action, He will be with them to help them accomplish the task.

IT'S ONLY THE PIANO!

Years ago, our church's worship pianist discovered that her husband had cancer. In order to care for him, she had to step aside. I'd never played lead piano before, and I was terrified to step up to the new position. One day, while I was practicing, I laid my head on the piano and asked God, crying. "Should I take this on?"

I seemed to hear Him whisper. "I made you for this." I called our pastor and volunteered. As a result, I played on the worship team for ten years!

Jeremiah 1

DAY FOUR

MOVING DEEPER IN THE CALL

In Jeremiah 1:9, God amplifies Jeremiah's calling. What additional facts does He reveal?

____

____

God wants to equip Jeremiah for his task. What does He give him?

____

This pattern is also repeated in numerous places in Scripture. When God calls His people out of Egypt, He gives them Moses. When God calls Moses to build the Tabernacle, God gives him skilled men and women to accomplish the task. When Solomon builds the temple, God gives him a master craftsman who works with metals and wood and stone. When God asks us to participate, He provides everything we need to get the job done.

In Jeremiah's case, he is called to speak for God. In order to fulfill the call, God gives Jeremiah the very words he will need to obey. One of the things we will observe as we progress through the book of Jeremiah is the continued refining and clarification of Jeremiah's call. At first, God tells Jeremiah only that he has been appointed a spokesman. In verse ten, God amplifies this, telling the young prophet exactly who will be in his audience. God says that Jeremiah will speak to nations and kingdoms. Though as yet, God has not been more specific than this, we can surmise that this is no small-time job that God has in mind.

In verses 11 and 13 Jeremiah tells God that he sees something. What does he see? (Note that in Hebrew, the word for "almond" sounds similar to the Hebrew word for "watching.")

Who seems to be the author of these visions? How does God interact with Jeremiah about the visions?

Read the story that begins in verse Acts 10:9. Here Peter experiences his own vision. Can you identify a pattern here?

While we certainly wouldn't use this passage to make a "vision doctrine," I love to recognize the ways that the God of the Old Testament is consistent with the God of the New Testament. Both Jeremiah and Peter experienced God's instruction through a vision. These two men were not left to question the meaning of their vision. They did not have to explain it using human imagination. In the midst of their vision, both men were aware of God explaining the exact meaning of what they saw. Sometimes, with God, a picture is worth a thousand words!

Jeremiah's vision gives us the first inkling of the source of God's coming punishment. Where will the trouble come from? What will they do when they arrive in the land of Judah?

In Jeremiah 1:16, God expresses, for the very first time, His complaint against His people. If this were the record of a modern trial, we might hear the judge say, "You are hereby charged with the crime of ____. How do you plead?" In this case, what is the primary charge (or charges) God brings against His people?

This two-fold charge will be repeated over and over throughout the Book of Jeremiah. In fact, the two charges are nearly always linked together every time they are mentioned. It seems that this crucial error involves a two-step process. The first step involves abandoning God. The second step involves turning to other gods. No matter what it is called, forsaking the fountain of living water, rebelling against God, abandoning God's instructions, the first step involves turning away from what you know to be right. This makes the second step easier. After abandoning right, the natural progression is to turn to what you know is wrong. Watch God refer to this same two-step process over and over throughout our study.

God ends the first chapter of Jeremiah (verse 17) by clarifying Jeremiah's call more specifically. Below, write the call given in verse 5. Then write the expanded call of verse 7. Last, make a list of the additional details in verses 17–18.

"This is my command—be strong and courageous! Do not be afraid or discouraged. For the Lord your God is with you wherever you go."

Joshua 1:9

Why do you think that God chose to repeat and expand? What did this accomplish? What might this tell you about God?

Jeremiah 1

DAY FIVE

GOD ADDRESSES JEREMIAH'S DOUBTS

In Jeremiah 1:17 God addresses Jeremiah's emotions for the second time. What does that tell you about Jeremiah? What effect might God's words have had on the young prophet?

In verse 18, God mentions four people who will not be able to stand against Jeremiah. (Pay careful attention to this list. By the end of the study, you will discover that these are exactly the people who rebel against Jeremiah's ministry) Make a note of the four people God mentions. Underline or highlight these four people in your Bible. Remember these as Jeremiah endures suffering for the sake of his calling.

"God answered, 'I will be with you. And this is your sign that I am the one who has sent you: When you have brought the people out of Egypt, you will worship God at this very mountain.'"
Exodus 3:12

Fear is a pretty common emotion. In the United States, our fears about ministry have to do mostly with failure and reputation. We worry about looking like a fool. We don't want to fall flat after we tell our friends about our new calling from the Lord. But Jeremiah had more substantive fears. In his day, calling the people to repentance might have a much higher cost. He might suffer humiliation, punishment, imprisonment, or even death.

But God gives Jeremiah a significant promise.

If Jeremiah will be courageous, God tells him that he will be like a fortified city that cannot be captured. What qualities make a fortified city safe? How might Jeremiah be like that?

When I think of a fortified city, I think of tall, thick walls, strong enough to keep my enemies outside. I think of strong gates that let food and goods come in and keep danger out. I think of watchtowers, where guardsmen keep watch over the city. I think of guards whose job is to protect the citizens of the town. This picture helps me envision God's protection in my life. He does the same here for Jeremiah, keeping him safe from his enemies, watching over him, and blessing him.

Perhaps the most important promise given in the entire chapter is found in Jeremiah 1:19. Why do you think that God chose to repeat this promise again at the end of chapter one?

___

___

___

ANCIENT FORTIFICATIONS

In Turkey, one ancient city has fortification walls thicker than the length of a modern city bus.

Now that, Jeremiah, is a fortified city!

As I Follow God:
As you close this lesson, you might want to make a list. Begin by taking a sheet of paper, and list the important areas of your life: Personal, Professional, Ministry, Finances, Family, Fitness, Discipline, etc. Under these categories, write down the ways our culture defines success.

For instance, in your family life, success might include factors like a happy marriage, well-behaved, moral children, children who marry well, or children who get a good education and have prosperous jobs. In our professional lives, we might define success as earning lots of money or having lots of influence or power. Perhaps it is climbing the ladder of responsibility, having impressive titles or winning awards. In fitness, success might include being thin, having chisled abs or having slim, muscular arms. Be sure to include worldly viewpoints as well as those of the Church along with your personal definitions of success.

Now take a close look at the list you have made. Is it possible, despite the ways our driven world has influenced our thinking, that God has a completely different definition of success? Do you see that in the first chapter of Jeremiah?

In our world, the drive for success appears even to have invaded the church. We judge our pastors by numbers—asking questions like: "How many members do you have?" "How many new believers?" "How many people attend your weekend services?" We judge Christian authors by their sales figures, evangelists by the size of their audience, speakers by the number of events they keynote every year, outreaches by the number of contacts made.

Even in the church, we sometimes find ourselves driven to attain outward measures of success.

It fascinates me that God called Jeremiah to a ministry that would not succeed. By any modern measure, Jeremiah was a failure. He was called to bring his own people to repentance, but they would not repent. He was called to turn the course of world events, to save Jerusalem from destruction. But Jerusalem was destroyed. He was called to keep the remnant from fleeing to Egypt. Yet they went anyway.

By these measures, Jeremiah failed.

But by the measure of faithful obedience, Jeremiah was a complete success.

He did what God called him to do, without giving up. Oh that I would learn to think like this! Oh that I would care only about obedience, not results. Oh that I could shed the expectations of the world, and begin to view success as God does!

Have you ever felt the Lord call you to a specific task? It might have been something big—starting a ministry, confronting a wrong, or even going back to school. Or, it might have been something that seemed unimportant at the time—prayer for a stranger, an encouraging phone call, or bringing dinner to a grieving friend. Did you struggle with your emotions, just like Jeremiah?

I have.

Fear is perhaps the most common emotion in every minister's heart. After I hear from God, I've often found myself muttering, "What are you thinking, God? I can't do this!"

Perhaps the job is too big, or I'm too inexperienced. Sometimes I worry that the request will take too long, or require too much energy. Perhaps I will experience rejection, humiliation. Perhaps, in my heart of hearts, I don't think I can succeed. Or worse, I don't want to obey. As doubts assail me, I take comfort in Jeremiah's story.

Like me, he struggled with insecurity. He didn't think people would listen—after all, he was just a kid. He was afraid of stepping out. What if the King decided to strike back? What if the other priests ostracized him? Surely people would ridicule him.

Jeremiah didn't think he could take the abuse.

Sometimes, I don't think so either. I'm so afraid of failure, rejection, and gossip that I try to sneak my way out of God's calling. I've been known to hide at home, hoping that no one will ask anything of me.

And then I remember that in the darkness of my mother's womb, God's hands formed me as well. I've been perfectly matched for and divinely appointed to my calling. Jesus promised He would be with me, even unto the end of the age. He has taught me that if God is for me, no one can stand against me.

God teaches that in obedience, there can be no failure—no matter what others think.

And when I call these things to mind, like Jeremiah and so many others after him, I find the courage to obey.

Do you?

Jeremiah 2–5

Refreshing the Soul

Once, years ago, I wrote a novel because God told me to. Seems like a pretty bold statement, doesn't it? No, I didn't hear an audible voice. Instead, I had a subject matter that I just couldn't seem to put out of my mind. I knew it would be a tough sell in the Christian Booksellers Association (CBA) market, but I couldn't shake the idea.

I knew it would be a tough sell in the Christian Booksellers Association (CBA) market, but I couldn't shake the idea.

I talked with my literary agent about selling the project. He hesitated. "I hate to put the brakes on your creativity. After all, you should write what God is telling you to write," he said. "But truthfully, I don't think I can sell it."

The funny thing is, I completely agreed with him. Why write what I couldn't publish? I put the idea out of my mind. But before long, it was back, tickling my imagination and demanding my attention. I prayed about it and asked for advice from fellow writers. Before long, I knew that I needed to follow through.

I tried to plot the story in a way that might be more publicly acceptable. I drove to Portland, nearly three hundred miles away, asking a friend for help. When I arrived home from the trip, I sensed the Holy Spirit telling me. *Write the book I asked you to write.* I had to call my friend and tell her that I couldn't write the story as we'd plotted it.

Eventually, I wrote exactly as I felt God was leading me. After some months, my agent sold the book to an enthusiastic publisher who released it a year later. Those who read it were astounded by the story (which even this many years later, still makes me cry). But in spite of the response, the novel didn't sell very many copies. Not long after its release, the publisher took it out of print.

I was devastated. How could my act of obedience garner anything less than commercial success? After all, I'd listened to the Holy Spirit and tried to obey. I'd persevered, in spite of advice to the contrary. Shouldn't book sales reflect that effort?

I slid into a depression of sorts. Only the sound advice and faithful prayer of many friends convinced me to look at the ways I was twisting truth. While God promises blessing for obedience, we sometimes make foolish assumptions about what exactly constitutes a blessing. I had presumed that God would bless book sales.

And the most painful part of the story? I learned that my writing life had become an idol of sorts. I had begun to take more satisfaction from sales and reviews than I did from my relationship with my creator. I had begun to obey *because of the blessing*, rather than obeying because of my love for my Savior.

I had a lot of repenting to do. And of course, with repentance came freedom from the sadness of a book taken out of print.

It's easy, isn't it, to let good, even wholesome things become the well from which we draw our happiness? Whenever we allow the opinions of others, our physical attractiveness, our money, our influence, our power, our popularity, or any other good thing, to become our sole source of refreshment, we trade God's genuine life-giving sustenance for a handful of sand.

It's a little like centering your diet on high-sugar foods. While some people can eat these things without any apparent effect, most of us can't. For every empty sugar calorie we eat, we deny ourselves the genuine nutrition—vitamins, minerals, micronutrients and fiber—contained in real food.

Every time we draw from the empty well of idolatry, we deny ourselves the life-giving sustenance of the fountain of living water.

Which path will you choose? Will you seek the fountain of life?

Jeremiah 2–5

DAY ONE

A Strong Beginning

In the world of fiction, most writers spend a lot of time thinking about point-of-view. They want to make certain that their story is told from the best possible perspective so that the reader is given all the information he needs to follow the plot complications.

Writers care about suspense. They want readers to know just enough so that they anticipate and worry about the hero's upcoming difficulty—but never so much that they become bored. In fiction writing, we want our readers to feel compelled to turn page after page, always desperate to see what happens next! Novelists like Tom Clancy and Ted Dekker include multiple point-of-view characters. In these novels, suspense is heightened because readers know what is happening to multiple people in multiple places at the same time. These details let the reader in on secrets the hero does not anticipate. We keep reading because we know what is coming and experience building anxiety about the hero's ability to cope with the upcoming disaster.

Other storytellers choose to restrict their story's point-of-view to a single character, forcing the reader to experience exactly what the character experiences, feeling his feelings as the story unfolds around him. This technique works because the reader is as blind as the hero. We feel the hero's anxiety. Like the hero, we don't know how it will all turn out. We get the clues at the same time he does, putting the story together one piece at a time.

Jeremiah is this kind of story.

The author, in this case, Jeremiah himself, chooses the most intimate of story modes. He tells his story in the first person, using phrases like this: "The Lord gave me another message." Because of this, we are completely caught in Jeremiah's world, unaware of the future, wondering what his enemies have planned, suspended in the danger of the moment. We are forced to walk in Jeremiah's shoes.

Most scholars agree that the book of Jeremiah was not written chronologically. It seems that Jeremiah organized the book with some other plan in mind. The story itself suggests that Jeremiah wrote several drafts. We know that at least one copy was destroyed when the king burned the text Jeremiah had given him through his secretary, Baruch.

In general, the first half of the book concentrates on God's messages to Judah. The middle quarter concentrates on God's messages to the Gentile world. And the last section reflects Jeremiah's experience, as God's judgments begin to unfold in Jerusalem.

These early chapters—the series of his sermons to the people of Judah—are frequently interrupted by Jeremiah's own reflections and by God's personal instructions to the prophet himself.

Interestingly, the sins committed by God's people 2,700 years ago reflect struggles very much like those of contemporary believers. As part of this week's study, use the chart on the next page to begin a list. In the first column, under "Sins of the Israelites," keep a running list of the charges God brings against His people. In the second column, labeled "21st century sins," try to visualize a corresponding sin that tempts 21st century believers. I think you'll be surprised at how similar people can be. It seems that time has not changed human nature. Throughout your study, you'll want to keep returning to this page, adding to your notes.

"For my people have done two evil things: They have forsaken me, the fountain of living water. And they have built for themselves cracked cisterns that can hold no water at all."

Jeremiah 2:13

Sins of the Israelites	Twenty-First Century Sins

This week, we'll be focusing on Jeremiah chapters two through six. You may read them all in one sitting or as you answer the following questions. Take as much time as you need to think through your questions. Ponder. Pray.

After reminding Judah of the people's early love in Jeremiah 2:2, God builds His case against His people. What three qualities exemplified their early commitment to God? What picture does God use to help us see this relationship?

____

____

____

____

____

APPLY When I first came to Christ, I lived in a University of Washington sorority. During those first days of faith, my housemates accused me of having a new boyfriend. In a way they were absolutely right! Looking back on your walk with God, do you remember your early fervor? What specifically did that look like? Can you describe some of the qualities of young love?

____

____

____

____

____

____

I have to laugh when I think about my early love for my husband. In those days, he was all I could talk about. My friends got tired of it very quickly. Before every date, I dressed carefully, going back and forth over every choice, even down to my selection of fragrance. I wanted to please my husband with my appearance, my kindness, my thoughtfulness. Judah was like that too. She wanted to please her God, the object of her sole affection. God tells us that she was quick to follow His lead, even into the wilderness, and that she was full of love for Him. Surprising, isn't it, how quickly she had abandoned her love for God?

This abandonment is amplified in Jeremiah 2:6–11, where the prophet speaks about how far the people have gone in their idol worship. They did not remember the God who delivered them from the wilderness. They did not appreciate the fruitful land God had given them. Even their leaders had ignored God, or prophesied nonsense in the name of an idol.

In verse 10, God chastises His people, essentially asking, "Has anyone anywhere ever been so strange as to exchange its glorious God for a worthless idol?"

In Jeremiah 2:5, God warns Judah about the consequences of idol worship. What happens to those who worship foolish idols?

____

____

COPING PROPERLY

"Jimmy" has an eating disorder. When life gets tough, he heads for the fridge. In one vulnerable moment, he wrote me about eating far beyond satisfaction. Unable to quit, yet so full that he could hardly stand the pain, he gorged himself with one food after another. "I knew that it wasn't the food that I wanted. It was something else. Something I couldn't even find words for. But I couldn't stop eating."

Though my friend is a believer, he had let food become a salve for his emotional wounds. Over the course of many years, the pattern became so entrenched that he grew to weigh over four hundred pounds. Eventually, with professional help and the prayer of his friends, Jimmy has learned other ways to cope with pain. His body now reflects the changes he has made in his heart. At last, Jimmy has learned to let God help him deal with the pain of life.

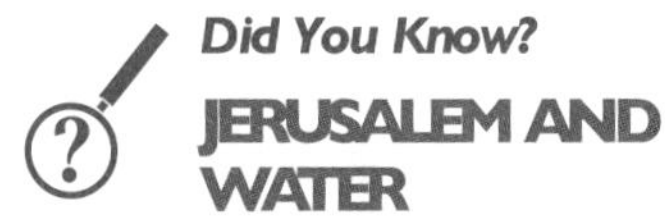

Did You Know? JERUSALEM AND WATER

In all of life, survival depends on water. Nowhere is this more powerfully illustrated than the Middle East, where little rainfall and few natural water resources challenge the most determined residents. Here, human life depends on the ability to collect and store water.

Jerusalem is no exception. With an annual rainfall of less than 22 inches, the city—situated in the southern hills of Palestine—has no natural aquifer beneath it. Only the Gihon Spring, which bubbles to the earth's surface in the Kidron Valley, east of the city, provides water for Jerusalem.

The city's livelihood has always depended on a single source of fresh water.

In Jeremiah 2:14 God mentions Israel. In this reference, Israel refers to the Northern Kingdom. What has happened to these people? Why?

____

____

____

Don't forget your Bible history. When the book of Jeremiah opens, the people of the Southern Kingdom are the only remnants of God's people remaining in the Promised Land. Most of the Northern Kingdom has been deported to Assyria, and Assyrians have replaced the deportees with its own people. God is using this bit of recent history to remind Jeremiah's audience that rebellion against God has a consequence. Only recently, Judah had seen it happen. What happened to the Northern Kingdom could and would happen to the Southern Kingdom—unless the people changed their ways.

In the New Living Translation, Jeremiah 2:17 reads this way: *"And you have brought this on yourselves by rebelling against the LORD your God when he wanted to lead you and show you the way."* This words imply that God has something He wants to do for us. What is it?

____

____

In the King James and the New American Standard versions, verse 17 is translated, *"When He led you in the way."* No matter what version you read, the implication is clear. God desires to and does lead us in the way we should go. He makes our path clear for us and allows us to choose whether or not we will follow the way.

Jeremiah 2–5

DAY TWO

A CONFLICT BREWS

Normally, the simplest of conflicts can be resolved in two stages. First there is the accusation. The offended party begins with an explanation of the difficulty. "This is what you have done," the accuser says, "and this is how it has affected me."

When everything is going well, the offender responds with understanding and sorrow. He might add something appropriate, like, "I'm sorry. I won't ever do that again." Occasionally, the two parties need to take more time to share their perspectives, each listening carefully to the other's explanation of the difficulty. Yesterday, as we looked at Jeremiah 2, we noted that God uses Jeremiah to bring serious charges against His people. Today, we are going to explore how the people respond.

Did You Know? CISTERNS

Throughout ancient history, citizens of the Middle East built cisterns to catch and hold rainwater. Most were long, narrow, and quite deep. The shape exposed a smaller surface area, thus preventing evaporation. Most featured arched rocks that supported a ceiling. This design protected vital water resources from the brutal heat of the desert sun.

In parts of the Middle East, the ability to store water enabled entire cultures to overcome the dangers of desert life and rise to civilization.

How does Judah respond to God in Jeremiah 2:23?

____

____

Judah's response seems to me a little like an adulterer who denies having an affair. These days, some spouses hire private investigators to prove their cases.

📖 In Jeremiah 2:26–28, what evidence does God bring to prove His accusation?

____

____

It seems hard to believe that God's people can call an image made of wood, "Father," or an idol chiseled from stone, "Mother." But apparently this is how far Judah had fallen. Still, we know that they understand what they are doing, because when times get tough, where do they go for help? They cry out to God, "Save us!" This very ambivalence seems to further condemn them.

📖 How long has this situation been going on (see Jeremiah 2:32)?

____

It seems that idolatry has led to other more serious sins. Can you name one? What might be the relationship between idolatry and this sin (2:33–35)? In the last sentence of this section, God connects the severe punishment, which is about to occur, with the claims Judah makes. What is her claim?

____

____

Sometimes, it is difficult to see where one sin leads to another. At first glance, idol worship would seem to have nothing at all to do with murder. But as you think about this depreciation in values, it makes sense. When we worship an idol instead of a living God, we set ourselves free from God's holy expectations. Once that happens, anything at all becomes acceptable, even murder.

📖 Look at Hebrews 12:5–11. What does this passage tell us about God's correction? What kind of person does God correct? What can we conclude about God's relationship with us, if we are being disciplined? When we experience discipline what should be our attitude? How does this compare with Jeremiah's audience?

____

____

____

____

____

God's Heart Revealed

Jeremiah 2–5

DAY THREE

In Jeremiah 3:1, God refers to an Old Testament law, which says a divorced man is not to remarry his wife after she has married another man. God uses this law to illustrate His deep and undying love for His people. In spite of Judah's adultery, God wants her (the Southern Kingdom) to return to Him. Even though the law does not require a man to remarry his wayward wife, God loves His wayward people so much that He is willing, even eager to have them back. How deep and committed is His love for His people!

Did You Know?
THE ASSYRIAN EMPIRE

According to expert historians, when Assyria conquered Israel's northern tribes, the empire was already nearly two thousand years old. A technically advanced empire, she boasted paved roads, the use of iron, plumbing, flush toilets, musical notation, a postal system and aqueducts.

Based in the common corners of modern Iraq, Syria, Turkey, and Iran, the Assyrians lived in the fertile breadbasket of ancient Mesopotamia. Well-watered fields supplied enough food to support a growing empire and vast army. Israel fell under the greedy eye of the Assyrians who wanted increased wealth and expanded trade. The Northern Tribes (and their capital Samaria) were conquered in 722 BC.

(http://www.assyriafoundation.org/ancient_history.html).

What example does God provide as a warning to Judah (Jeremiah 3:6–10)? In this passage, the word "Israel" refers to the Northern Kingdom. Does Judah respond? (You'll find more information about this in the sidebar about the Assyrian empire and the Assyrian captivity.)

It is true that God often provides other people's experiences to show us the consequence of sin. In fact, the New Testament claims that the entire account of the Old Testament is given for our instruction. If Judah had taken Israel's punishment seriously, its people would have repented, cleared the land of idols, and perhaps even redoubled their commitment to the covenant they had made with God. Unfortunately, they watched Assyria defeat Israel, and shrugged.

"Oh well," they seemed to say. "Too bad for them."

In Jeremiah 3:11–15, God makes a series of requests. List the requests in the space below. If the people choose God's way, what does He promise (Jeremiah 3:22)? Have you ever felt as if your heart had a wayward tendency? What does this passage teach you about God's desire for the wayward?

I have a friend who knows me very well. She senses when I have a bad attitude. When she feels my heart begin to harden, she prays for me like this: "Lord, help my friend *want* to repent. Help her *want* to be sorry." It always makes me laugh when I hear her pray. But she is completely correct in her approach. Sometimes, when we are rejecting God's truth, we need to take a step back. God can help us desire to do what we know is right, even in the midst of angry or hurt feelings, even when we want to retaliate rather than forgive. And when we ask, He is willing to correct our negative attitude and heal our wayward hearts.

"So he returned home to his father. And while he was still a long way off, his father saw him coming. Filled with love and compassion, he ran to his son, embraced him, and kissed him."

Luke 15:20

📖 Read the story of the Prodigal Son in Luke 15:11–31. Here Jesus gives us a practical picture of what repentance might actually look like. When the son returns to his father, what does he do? Are these things similar to the requests God makes of Judah in Jeremiah? How?

My New Living Translation uses these words in the list of God's instructions to his people. *Come home* (to me). *Acknowledge* (your guilt). *Admit* (your rebellion). *Confess* (your refusal to follow me). You might not be struck by those verbs, but I find it interesting how similar they are to the actions of the Prodigal son. While the hungry son is out feeding the pigs, he recognizes his foolishness and plans his confession to his father. He returns home. When he arrives, he admits his folly and confesses his sins once again.

Apparently, starting over with God depends on our ability to turn back, acknowledge, admit, and confess. God wants us to grow in our ability to admit fault. After all, we can't change direction until we admit that we are off course!

A Repentant Heart

Jeremiah 2–5

DAY FOUR

Jeremiah 4 opens with another three-part request and promise. Note the details of the Lord's proposal. Begin with the requests:

____

____

____

____

What promise does God make?

____

____

In fiction, we have a rule: "Show, don't tell." By this we mean that we want our character's actions to show the reader what the character is like. For example, we don't tell the reader that the hero is generous; instead, we show him giving away his only coat to a homeless man. We want to supply the evidence and let the reader decide.

I find it interesting that God seems to operate by the same standards. He is unsatisfied with simple confession. He wants more from His people than just admission. He wants change. It isn't enough to confess idolatry. Confession must be reinforced by action. Throw away the idols! Live good, holy, God-fearing lives. If you will turn to the living God, you must begin to live according to His standards.

For fun, consider Jeremiah 4:3 in several different translations. If this verse is actually a means to an end, what would be the "means" (the methods), and what would be the "end" (the desired result)? In practical terms how would **you** plow up the hard ground of your own heart?

____

____

____

____

I think believers often use prayer as a catchall solution for every problem. Don't get me wrong. Prayer is always the **best** starting point for every problem. But few of us use the power of prayer to its full advantage. Some folks never begin to pray because they know their attitude isn't right. They believe they must somehow conform before they ask God for help. Isn't prayer—like the prayer of my friend when my attitude has soured—our very access to the power of the Holy Spirit to bring change?

Did You Know?
ROOTS OF RACIAL TENSION

The Assyrians quelled rebellion in conquered lands by a systematized transplantation system. Members of the overthrown population were deported to the Assyrian homeland, while at the same time, Assyrian natives then moved to the conquered land. Eventually these Assyrians intermarried with the indigenous people creating new bloodlines, permanently uniting the conquered with their conquerors.

Mosaic law forbid intermarriage between Jews and non-Jews. So, in the case of the Northern Tribes, this system of Assyrian transplantation effectively "polluted" the pure blood of the Jewish people, causing a deep schism between the racially pure Jewish people (in the Southern Kingdom) and this mixed-breed, which became known as "Samaritans" (from the name of the capital, Samaria). Scholars believe this is the root of the hatred between Jews and Samaritans evidenced in the New Testament account of the Woman at the Well and the parable of the Good Samaritan.

SOMETHING TO THINK ABOUT

Yes, they knew God, but they wouldn't worship him as God or even give him thanks. And they began to think up foolish ideas of what God was like. As a result, their minds became dark and confused. Claiming to be wise, they instead became utter fools. And instead of worshiping the glorious, ever-living God, they worshiped idols made to look like mere people and birds and animals and reptiles. (Romans 1:21–23)

Sometimes, we must plow up the hard ground of our own heart. I sometimes soften my hard heart with music. Sometimes with tears. Sometimes with exercise, walking, or biking until I can hardly breathe and sob at the same time. These things are most effective when peppered with constant and deeply honest prayer. Like David, the writer of many psalms, I often start with angry and accusing prayers and with God's help, I end up somewhere completely different.

The people of Judah weren't the only ones to suffer from hard-heartedness. It's a common ailment. It's good practice, learning to farm the hard ground of your own heart.

Some people maintain that God never feels anger when dealing with His people. Using several different translations of Jeremiah 4:4 how would you answer that charge?

____

____

I love to think about God's emotions. Though some believers don't realize it, God has a full range of emotions, including anger. In fact, our emotions often reflect His own. After all, we are created in His image! You will find these emotions illustrated—some directly, some more subtly—all through the pages of the Old and New Testaments.

📖 In Jeremiah 4:22, God gives the root causes for His people's current circumstances. What are those causes? Was it fair of God to expect this of people who had so little access to written scriptures to guide them?

____

____

____

____

If knowing God short-circuits foolishness and senselessness, then how do you think these pre-Bible people might have come to know God? How do *you* go about knowing God? What New Testament scriptures come to mind in your quest to know God?

____

____

____

____

In Colossians 1, Paul mentions a cycle that should occur regularly in every believer's life. In verse 9, Paul says the cycle begins with knowing God's will for our lives. Then, God gives us the wisdom we need to obey His will. Next we obey, taking whatever steps God shows us to take. The cycle is complete as our obedience helps us to know God more deeply.

Here is a practical example: In His Word, God tells us that all believers should meet regularly with other believers. But the Bible doesn't tell us specifically which church to join or which Bible study to attend. As we strive to obey, his Holy Spirit gives us the wisdom we need to find the right church, or home group, or Bible study. And we obey. As the process unfolds, we have grown in our understanding of God and in our ability to hear Him guide us. As we follow Him, we grow ever more intimate with the God that we follow.

As we come to know Him more—His enabling power, His provision, His deepest desire for our lives—He shows us His will for us and we begin the cycle of obedience all over again, always growing more deeply in the knowledge of God. As you think about this cycle, has your answer to the last question, "How do pre-Bible people come to know God?" changed?

____

____

What challenge does God make in Jeremiah 5:1? What does this challenge tell you about how serious the problem in Jerusalem actually is? Compare this simple verse to Genesis 18:31. What do these two scriptures tell you about God's nature, especially as it relates to punishment?

____

____

____

____

God's divine nature is clearly revealed in Scripture. Notice Jesus' words in Matthew 18:14. After the story of the lost sheep, He concludes, *"In the same way, it is not my heavenly Father's will that even one of these little ones should perish."* We know that the story is not really about sheep, but about the heart of the Good Shepherd, who is willing to search high and low for the one lost sheep. The Good Shepherd has no desire that any of us should perish.

This same value is reflected in Jeremiah. God simply does not wish that any of His children experience punishment. While I wouldn't base doctrine on any one scripture passage, I can see from these many passages that God does not delight in punishing His people. In fact, it seems to me that He longs to avoid it.

According to Jeremiah, the poor and ignorant shouldn't be expected to know the ways of the Lord (5:4). So, Jeremiah looks to the leaders—the priests, prophets, and king. What did Jeremiah discover about the leaders of the people?

____

____

God's Discipline

Jeremiah 2–5

DAY FIVE

In Jeremiah 5:15–17, God describes the coming army. List the details he mentions here:

____

____

APPLY In Jeremiah 5:23, God describes the people's hearts. What two adjectives does He use? Can you think of a time that God might have used these adjectives to describe you? What are you doing to prevent developing this kind of heart?

In Jeremiah 5:23, God says, *"They do not say from the heart, 'Let us live in awe of the LORD our God, for he gives us rain each spring and fall, assuring us of plentiful harvests.'"* In this simple statement, I think God may have given us a key to living in awe of Him. Perhaps by living in conscious awareness of His provision, in continual gratitude, we can begin to live in awe of God.

📖 What wicked deeds does God describe in Jeremiah 5:26–29? How do these sins compare to the behavior of the church? Of our culture or community?

In my home group, one of our members has experienced a recent opportunity. His company has placed their its sales leader in his department. This sales leader has been instructed to train the sales team in all of his skills. Unfortunately for my friend, not all of these skills reflect integrity or honesty. While my friend acknowledges that he has much to learn, he is clearly unwilling to adopt all of the sales leader's practices. As the scripture in Jeremiah implies, this salesman thinks of sales as a way to lie in wait for victims. In Jeremiah's Jerusalem, this sales leader would have fit right in.

In modern Christian culture, what constitutes success? Does that definition match your own?

📖 In Jeremiah 5:30–31 what do the people enjoy (like, or take pleasure in)?

God continues to warn His people, begging them to change course. However, in these last verses of chapter 5, God tells us how much it will cost His people to change their ways. They will have to rebel against leaders who lead them down the wrong path. They will have to ignore the rules and regulations of priests and prophets.

Remember that chapter and verse divisions are modern inventions for our own convenience. The quote at the end of Chapter 5 continues into Chapter 6. Yet, God ends Chapter 5 with this question, *"But what will you do when the end comes?"* This brings us to an important reflection.

📖 Looking at these passages in Jeremiah 3:1, 12–13; 4:1–2; 6:8, do you think destruction of Jerusalem was set in stone? Or, might something have changed the course of history? How might that have looked? Can you think of another biblical example?

As I consider these verses, I cannot help but think of the prophet Jonah. Late in his story, Jonah reveals his concern about accepting his assignment to preach in Nineveh, saying, *"Didn't I say before I left home that you would do this, LORD? That is why I ran away to Tarshish! I knew that you are a merciful and compassionate God, slow to get angry and filled with unfailing love. I knew how easily you could cancel your plans for destroying these people"* (Jonah 4:2).

In Jonah's case, when he finally preached in Nineveh, the people marvelously responded. They repented. And their sincere repentance turned back God's punishment. Jonah knew it. We know it. God doesn't want to punish us, but if we refuse to repent He will.

In Romans 2:4, we read, *"Don't you realize how kind, tolerant and patient God is with you? Or, don't you care? Can't you see how kind he has been in giving you time to turn from your sin?"*

As I Follow God:
It would be easy, while studying these chapters, to get lost in the lists. After all, God spends a lot of time telling His people—through Jeremiah—about the mistakes they've made. They worshiped idols, yet still expected God to save them from their enemies. They killed the innocent and the poor, yet felt no remorse. They trusted in political allies rather than in the God of their fathers. They had forgotten God and wandered far from Him. They watched their northern neighbors in Israel suffer the punishment for these same sins, and yet they believed they would somehow escape God's judgment. All were foolish and refused to know God.

The good thing about lists is that we can check them off; it feels good to think that we haven't made the same mistakes as those foolish people in Jeremiah's audience. I've never worshiped an idol. Check. I've never killed the innocent or the poor. Check. As long as my checklist stays clean, I can begin to feel pretty pleased with my own spiritual condition.

Until I trip over Jeremiah 2:13, *"For my people have done two evil things: They have forsaken me—the fountain of living water. And they have dug for themselves cracked cisterns that can hold no water at all."*

God uses this vital, life-giving fluid as an illustration of the vital, life-giving relationship we must continually have with the LIVING God. As water is essential to survival, so God is essential to our life in the dry environment of the human soul. Without water, crops fail, animals die, topsoil blows away, and human life ends. Without God, human life has no meaning. Without Him, we cannot grow or flourish; we cannot bear fruit. Living without God brings certain death.

How often have I done the same thing as Jeremiah's people? How often have I turned away from the living God and sought my deepest gratification from other sources?

THE PERILS OF FAITH

But others trusted God and were tortured, preferring to die rather than turn from God and be free. They placed their hope in the resurrection to a better life. Some were mocked, and their backs were cut open with whips. Others were chained in dungeons. Some died by stoning, and some were sawed in half; others were killed with the sword... (Hebrews 11:35–36).

God uses a fountain to illustrate His own eternal, continually refreshing character. Think about an oasis. You've seen the pictures. In the middle of the desert, for some reason, a spring rises near enough to the ground's surface to support life. From miles away, across barren land, the oasis calls the traveler forward, to the fresh green of plant life, to food, to shade, to rest, and the miraculous rejuvenating power of water. As water restores the body, our relationship with God restores the soul. Why would we turn from that?

But God's people have turned from Him! And more than that, they have tried to replace Him. This would be like the people who live near an oasis, deciding not to return to the spring for water. Instead, they decide to dig a hole under the house where they will store the water they need. But the ground they trust won't hold water. It has a flaw. A leak. A crack. The water they try to store keeps seeping away into the ground.

Why would anyone do that? Convenience? Did they want to avoid the daily trip back to the fountain? Fear? Are they afraid that some day they'll head out to the fountain and discover that it is dry?

It's so easy to criticize, isn't it? That is, until you begin to see yourself in the passage. How often do I let the busy concerns of life—carpool, music lessons, choir practice, Sunday school preparations—keep me from the Fountain of Living Water? How often do I choose worry over prayer? How often do I head to the cookie jar to salve my wounded heart? How often do I choose television over the Word? How often do I choose my friend's advice over God's direction? When I remember my own weak heart, I realize that I'm not very different from Jeremiah's audience.

Not very different at all.

The first time I taught this study, I had my class make a list of the cisterns where they seek to salve their own wounded hearts. We listed things like rank, position, influence, money, success, satisfaction, comfort, intellect, education, possessions, adoration of others, approval, acceptance, clothes, appearance, and our scientific ability to overcome all obstacles by reason and intelligence.

Then we made a list of the cisterns where Christians try to store their life-giving refreshment. Surprisingly, the two lists weren't all that different. In fact, good things were on both lists: relationships, ministry, church membership, worship, service, even psychology.

Good things, when they become idols, become dangerous things. I have a friend who is dangerously close to letting her workout routine become an idol. Her life is in shambles. Her marriage needs attention. One of her children is living in a boarding school for troubled teens. What probably began as a coping mechanism has gained dangerous importance in her life.

I've known people for whom income has become an idol. I've struggled with letting book sales become my own idol. The truth is, that Christians, who should know better, also fall into the trap of seeking solace in cracked cisterns. We find refreshment in things other than God.

But instead of wallowing in guilt, I choose hope. I remind myself of how very often God invites His people to return. "Return to me," He says, over and over. And in Jeremiah 3:22, *"My wayward children,"* says the Lord, *"come back to me, and I will heal your wayward hearts."*

We should all take Jeremiah's admonition seriously. Are there things in your life that replace God's life-giving refreshment? Do you comfort yourself with food? Do you head to the gym while forsaking your prayer closet? Do you take excessive comfort in your accomplishments? Do you worry too much about what others think about you? I catch myself falling into these traps too!

But there is good news! The cure is simple; once the diagnosis is made, we must head straight to the healer of our soul. His water will cleanse us, refresh us, and make us new!

Spend some time today thinking about how you can draw life-giving water, from Jesus.

Notes

lesson 3

Jeremiah 6–9

Knowing God

Have you ever been misdiagnosed? I have. About one year after our youngest child was born, I went to the doctor complaining of pelvic pain. After a brief exam, my family practice doctor told me that I was just "too sensitive to my body." According to him, I was only feeling myself ovulate, nothing more.

JEREMIAH 9:24

But those who wish to boast should boast in this alone: that they truly know me and understand that I am the Lord who demonstrates unfailing love and who brings justice and righteousness to the earth, and that I delight in these things. I, the Lord, have spoken!

Confused and frustrated by the doctor's evaluation, I went home. Maybe nothing was wrong. Then again, maybe I was experiencing something more serious than his skills could detect.

Two months later, still struggling with pain, I sought another opinion. The second physician ordered an ultrasound, which revealed an ovarian cyst the size of a grapefruit. No wonder I had pain! It took more than two years of treatment and diagnosis to find out that I had Polycystic Ovarian Syndrome—a rare collection of symptoms and problems that plagued nearly every area of my life.

What my family practice doctor termed "oversensitivity" turned out to be something much more serious. My treatment required endless ultrasounds, close evaluation and management of my thyroid gland, blood sugars, and digestive tract. In the end, I had two separate surgeries to remove failing ovaries. My family doctor wanted to help; instead, he misdiagnosed. And, though the disease would never have proven fatal, with the right diagnosis, I might have gotten the right treatment more quickly.

This week, we'll watch as the people of Judah experience a misdiagnosis of their own. They have pain too—the threat of a mighty army invading from the North. Their capital, the city of Jerusalem, is crowded with people who have moved in from the country, desperate to save themselves from what appears to be imminent attack. Like me, these people are hearing two different diagnoses—one from their leaders and priests, and quite a different diagnosis from Jeremiah.

Jeremiah 6–9

DAY ONE

AN OVERVIEW OF THE TEXT

How would you feel about hearing conflicting messages? Would you be confused? Would you choose to believe the harder message? Would you ask for another opinion, or seek God for clarification? I like to think, considering the severity of the consequences facing Jeremiah's audience, that I would seek God.

But the people of Judah made a different choice. They closed their ears and buried their heads. They chose to believe the lies in spite of the evidence. Though they knew better, they hoped for the best. They continued life as it always was—reveling in the sins of their fathers and grandfathers. Thus, their own foolishness brought the world down around their ears.

In spite of Judah's stubborn resistance, Jeremiah gives contemporary believers a great example to follow. He shows us how to serve God wholeheartedly, even when no one listens. We'll learn a great deal from this young prophet.

This week, we'll also learn about the ways God communicates with people caught in sin. We'll look at the things that might trap contemporary believers into feeling proud. And, we'll consider the ways we fool ourselves into thinking we are safe in our sin. Finally, we'll take a look at the meaning of repentance.

I think you'll find compassion for the people of Judah. Though we live more than two thousand years later, we aren't so very different, really. It takes courage to face a tough diagnosis and do something about it. It takes the same kind of courage to face your own sin.

That kind of courage might have saved the people of Judah from their pain.

It will surely save you!

This week you face a long lesson with many questions. Don't let the workload discourage you! Many of these questions require only simple observations—nothing more than a one- or two-word answer. Try to pace yourself throughout the week so that you aren't overwhelmed.

We'll be covering Jeremiah, chapters six through nine this week. You might want to read these chapters in one sitting. Or, you can read one chapter at a time as you answer your questions.

📖 Jeremiah 6 opens with a warning. What is going to happen? Can you identify some details about the coming destruction? (Consider these age-old newspaper questions: Who? How? When?)

____

____

____

📖 Turn to Jeremiah 6:6, where God speaks these words, *"This is what the Lord Almighty says:"* It is his response to the description of this looming event. Why is the city to be destroyed?

____

____

📖 Apparently, God's people have moved from idolatry to complete wickedness. After many warnings, God is ready to do something about it. Observing the second half of Jeremiah 6:9, note God's picture of picking grapes from a vine. The New Living Translation uses the phrase *"gleaned again."* Thinking about the destruction of Jerusalem described in 2 Chronicles 36:5–7, and 36:17–20, to what might the idea of a second gleaning, or picking refer?

____

____

Twice in the book of Leviticus, God tells His people exactly how they must harvest their crops. The words of God are translated this way in the New International Version, *"When you reap the harvest of your land, do not reap to the very edges of your field or gather the gleanings of your harvest"* (Leviticus 19:9). The gleaning refers to the second combing of the fruit from the harvest. For instance if you are harvesting strawberries, the gleanings would refer to the strawberries not ripe during the first picking. God intended the second harvest, or gleaning, to be kept for the poor among His people.

In the case of Jerusalem, the term gleaning does not refer to those who receive the "fruit," but rather to the fact that there will be a second picking.

I find it completely amazing that God's warning is so specific. He tells His people that the enemy will come from the North, that the enemy will use siege tactics and will attack not just once, but more than once. All of these details are confirmed in later chapters of this book, as well as in the books of 2 Kings and 2 Chronicles.

In 2 Kings 24, this first picking of Jerusalem is described. Here, Nebuchadnezzar invades Judah and extracts a tribute from the king—demanding a price for leaving Jerusalem alone. You can remember this first invasion as the "Price Invasion."

The second invasion is described briefly beginning in 2 Kings 24:10. In this invasion, Nebuchadnezzar besieges the city of Jerusalem; King Jehoiakin, his advisors, nobles, and officials all surrender to the Babylonian king, who removes them to Babylon. You can remember this invasion as the "Prince Invasion." Nebuchadnezzar takes Judah's brightest young princes back to Babylon with him.

The third "gleaning," or invasion is the final one. At the time of Jeremiah 6,

Put Yourself in Their Shoes

WRONG DIAGNOSIS

In a 2004 story, ABC News* correspondent John McKenzie describes the difficulty Kathy Kastan had obtaining an accurate medical diagnosis. When she sought treatment for exceptional fatigue and dizziness brought on by exercise, three doctors failed to diagnose her condition. Eight months later she collapsed on a hiking trip and required emergency bypass surgery. Kathy had severe heart disease.

The statistics are frightening. Thirty-eight percent of women will die in the first year after a heart attack, while during the same period only twenty-five percent of men die. Scientists believe that women with heart disease and heart attacks have different symptoms than men, making emergency rooms more likely to misdiagnose their medical condition. In some cases, members of the medical staff refuse to take women's heart-related complaints seriously.

The people of Jerusalem had a deadly spiritual disease; but their doctors—the priests and prophets—continued to declare them well, saying "Peace, Peace," when in fact, they were only moments away from destruction.

*(http://abcnews.go.com/WNT/News/story?id=295352)

this invasion has yet to happen. However, God is predicting through Jeremiah that it will include the final destruction of the city. You can think of this invasion as a "Permanent Invasion" of the land.

Price. Prince. Permanent. Through Jeremiah, God gives a clear warning of exactly what will happen to the city of Jerusalem, unless her people repent. Remarkable, isn't it? God used the simple picture of a farmer gathering grapes to tell His people exactly what would happen in the not-too-distant future.

Why do you think God gives this level of detail to the people?

____

____

APPLY In Jeremiah 6:10, God describes the responsiveness of His people. Make a list of the ways God describes their condition. Are these descriptions different ways of saying the same thing, or do they have subtle differences in meaning? Have you ever found yourself in a similar place? When? Have you ever had a friend with closed ears? What did that look like?

____

____

____

____

You may disagree, but I wonder if these descriptions actually reveal different conditions. In the King James Version, the verse declares, *". . . behold the word of the Lord is unto them a reproach; they have no delight in it."* It is as if by choosing to reject God's word, His people then suffer from closed ears. Their choice has brought about their inability to hear.

In this section God makes additional charges against the leaders of His people (6:13–15). Who is it, and what have they done?

____

____

What seems to be the problem? Can you think of a contemporary correlation to these charges? (You might also look also at Jeremiah 8:10–11, 21–22.)

____

____

____

How sad that the very people who ought to be instructing and leading God's people are themselves deceived. The priests and prophets have become enamored with the same sins the people have embraced. They no longer lead the people to God; instead, they offer the people permission, even approval for continuing in sin.

Paul warns us of this very issue in Titus 2:1, *"As for you, promote the kind of living that reflects right teaching."* God has always required his leaders, be they priest (in the Old Testament), pastor, deacon, elder, or teacher (in the New Testament) to live God's truth.

In Jeremiah 6:16 what does God suggest that His people do? Write down the first three verbs you find in this verse. (Verbs are action words. If you list these separately, you will observe an interesting pattern.)

A Clearer Call

In Jeremiah 6:19, God says, *"Listen all the earth, I will bring disaster upon my people. It is the fruit of their own sin because they refuse to listen to me."* Why do you suppose that God wants all the earth to understand WHY the disaster is about to come?

In Jeremiah 6:27 God describes Jeremiah's role in this story in a new way. Of course, by earthly standards, Jeremiah's ministry might be considered a complete failure. He was called to turn the people from sin; but the people did not repent. In the space below, rewrite the phrase God uses when he speaks of Jeremiah's ministry:

Using your own words, and considering what we know is the end result of Jeremiah's ministry, try to explain this new perspective of Jeremiah's calling. How might this have differed from Jeremiah's perspective? How does this change your perspective of your own ministry?

In Jeremiah 6:28, God compares His people to the qualities of two metals. How are His people like these qualities?

When we were newly married, my husband Kim was in dental school. In order to supplement our income, he began building crowns for a nearby dentist. It was good practice for Kim and helped the other dentist be more productive.

Kim set up a tiny lab in our downstairs bathroom. One afternoon, I went down to visit with him. As I watched my husband heat the dental gold with a torch, it melted into a glowing liquid. Then, he took a small box and shook what looked like red pepper onto the metal. Sparks flew.

Did You Know?

ANCIENT SMELTING TECHNIQUES

Ancient silversmiths purified silver by hand, grinding silver ore (usually at least ten parts per million of silver) into a fine powder called slag. Then they heated the ore in the presence of an organic material and lead. The organic material (usually charcoal or wood) provided a high-carbon environment enabling the liquid lead to trickle down through the molten slag, picking up the silver particles along the way. The less-dense leftover rock and debris floated to the top of the mixture, while the silver-lead mixture sank to the bottom. The remainders were then skimmed or poured from the surface of the container.

In the second stage of refining, the solid lead-silver ingot is heated again in a bone-ash crucible. When the mixture reaches 900 degrees Centigrade, the lead oxidizes to a liquid, which is then absorbed by the porous bone-ash container. This temperature is not high enough to melt the silver. So, the silver remains in the bottom of the container in the form of a pure silver button, which is then removed, melted and used as needed.

The box carried the label, **Red Devil.**

"What is that?" I asked.

"It's a catalyst," he said. "I add it to the gold, and it creates a chemical reaction that drives out the impurities."

This is a little like Jeremiah's role in the city of Jerusalem. God has placed him there to determine the quality of God's people. However, in this case, Jeremiah cannot drive the impurity from the precious metal, because there is no precious metal in the mix.

The New Living Translation uses the phrase *"insolent as bronze."* Insolent means aggressively disrespectful. The people are apparently not just ignoring God, but perhaps even mocking in their disobedience. This is what contemporary audiences would call "in your face" disrespect. In their disrespect they have become hard and cruel as well. As iron is hard, so have God's people become stiff and unresponsive. Isn't this a sad commentary on the very people who—above all others—should be responsive toward God?

Jeremiah 6–9

DAY THREE

JEREMIAH CHAPTER 7

God speaks again in Jeremiah 7:3. What is required to avoid the coming deportation? God lists five things the people can do to show this change of heart. List four of them here:

____

____

____

____

____

Interesting, isn't it, that contemporary Christian recovery methods emphasize a very similar point. When people profess sorrow for their sins, be they sexual, food related, or addictive behaviors, experts advise that loved ones don't accept sorrow as being enough, in itself, to build renewed trust. Family members and dear friends are advised to wait for a visible change in behavior before risking renewed relationship with the recovering person.

In this way, modern counselors simply reflect God's standards. In essence, God advises, "Express your repentance in new behavior, and then I will believe that you have had a real change of heart."

From the words in Jeremiah 7:4, I'll bet you can guess what the "priests" are saying about Jeremiah's message? Share your ideas here.

____

____

____

Put Yourself in Their Shoes

TOUGH LOVE

When our children were very small, sometimes I had to discipline them in front of my husband's parents. While they never interfered, I knew it was painful for them to watch. More than once I caught tears glistening in my father-in-law's eyes.

"I know it has to be done," my husband's mother used to say, "but it hurts to hear them cry." She understood that children need correction when they willfully disobey the rules. Today, my in-laws are incredibly proud of their grown grandchildren. Do you think that Jeremiah's prayers might have been a little like a grandfather trying to stave off the discipline of his beloved grandchild? Might that be the reason God wanted Jeremiah to stop praying?

📖 In your own words, paraphrase Jeremiah 7:9–10.

____

____

____

These verses seem to imply that God's people felt safe because the Temple was built among them. After all, God would never allow an advancing army to destroy the Temple, would He? Jeremiah's audience believed they could do whatever they pleased, and then go to the Temple and be safe. In our modern Christian culture, is there something that we believers treat like a "temple of safety" when it comes to sin? For instance, have you ever known folks who thought they could live an immoral life and be safe from correction because they provided financial support to the church?

Can you think of other ways modern Christians avoid responsibility for sin, thinking they are safe because....

____

____

____

📖 In Jeremiah 7:16, God speaks to Jeremiah about his prayer life. What does God command him to stop doing?

____

The last half of verse 16 reads, *". . . don't beg me to help them for I will not listen to you."* What do you think—especially considering God's emotion in this situation—Jeremiah's prayer life might have looked like? Why do you think that God wants him to stop praying?

____

____

____

____

📖 In Jeremiah 7:19, God names the true victim of idolatry. Who is it?

____

Remember that in our last lesson, God tells His people that those who worship foolish idols become foolish themselves. God's instructions remain consistent here. Worshiping anything or anyone other than God only hurts the fool who does it.

📖 When God led Abraham's family out of Egypt, what was the **one thing** He asked of them (see Jeremiah 7:22)? In the 2,700 years since Jeremiah was written, do you think anything has changed?

____

____

Today, we don't follow Mosaic Law. We don't sacrifice animals or observe Old Testament festivals and holy days. Does God desire something more or

DISOBEDIENCE AND IDOLATRY

But Samuel replied, "What is more pleasing to the Lord: your burnt offerings and sacrifices or your obedience to his voice? Listen! Obedience is better than sacrifice, and submission is better than offering the fat of rams. Rebellion is as sinful as witchcraft, and stubbornness as bad as worshiping idols. So because you have rejected the command of the Lord, he has rejected you as king." (1 Samuel 15:22)

something different from us than what He asked of His people in the Old Testament? Why do you think so?

The New Testament is full of advice, commands, and admonitions. Let me list a few of them here: Get rid of all the evil in your lives (James 1). Devote yourselves to prayer (Colossians 4:2). You slave owners must be just and fair to your slaves (Colossians 4:1). Stay away from complaining and arguing (Philippians 2:14). Let there be no sexual immorality, impurity or greed among you (Ephesians 5:3). Don't get tired of doing good (Galatians 6:9). Pay your teachers (Galatians 6:6).

Since modern Christians don't obey Old Testament law, how do you think obedience and these New Testament commands might fit together?

In Jeremiah 7:25–26 God says He has sent His prophets, day in and day out. How do the people respond?

Verse 27 repeats the same theme, with different translations using the following phrases:

- *"refuse to be taught"* (NLT)
- *"did not accept correction"* (NASB)
- *"obeyeth not"* (KJV)

In the space below, reflect on what you think it means to be "teachable."

"I have loved you even as the Father has loved me. Remain in my love. When you obey my commandments, you remain in my love, just as I obey my Father's commandments and remain in his love."

John 15:9–10

Have you ever signed up for a class from a well-known instructor? Do you remember the thrill you felt as you anticipated a new skill or advanced training? Do you remember how excited you were when you walked into class? Did you take notes? Record the class? Buy a workbook?

As you think about this week's lesson, ask yourself the following questions:

Do you come to God with that same level of excitement, that same anticipation?

Do you listen as eagerly to His instruction?

Would you pay for the lessons He is teaching you?

Do you value His lessons as much as those you pay for?

Once again, in Jeremiah 7:30, God lists three specific evidences of Judah's idolatry. What are they?

(Optional: You can read more about the third example in Isaiah 57:5. Because Isaiah preached to Judah long before Jeremiah, we know this specific problem had been a longstanding one.) In Jeremiah 7:32–34, God responds to the people's actions. What response does He promise?

Thinking about Honesty

Jeremiah 6–9

DAY FOUR

In this week's lesson, I'd like you to see the ebb and flow of God's work with His people. God does not always approach His people in the same way. He is not always angry. He is not always blunt. He is not always gentle. In fact, in the Book of Jeremiah, we can see that God alternates between three techniques. He confronts His people with their sin, courts them with His love, and warns them of upcoming disaster. Notice the pattern as it continues through chapters 8 and 9.

Have you ever tried to help someone reconsider his choices? Perhaps you know people who have abandoned God's principles and started off on their own way. Perhaps they were thinking about giving up on God. Perhaps they were considering divorce or even adultery. Or maybe they were in the throws of anguish after a painful betrayal. Others might be in the midst of experiencing God's divine correction. I believe it would help us to remember God's pattern of reaching out to His people—variously confronting, courting, and warning—as you consider speaking with those who are struggling with sin. How might this pattern influence your approach with people you love?

Observe the text as God reverts to His teaching voice. In Jeremiah 8:4, God compares His people to people who start down the wrong road. When wise people discover their mistake, what do they do?

In turning back from sin, what does God expect to hear from His people (8:6)?

Instead, what does He hear?

It seems so simple doesn't it? If you were in a new city, trying to arrive at a function with nothing more than an address and simple directions, wouldn't you want to follow instructions? If you found that you had passed the street where you needed to turn, wouldn't you stop and turn around? If we can do this with directions, why do we have so much trouble stopping and turning around when it comes to God's Word?

Read Jeremiah 8:8–9 in a modern translation. Here, God brings an accusation against the teachers of the time. What does He say they have done?

APPLY Wouldn't it be tragic to think yourself a teacher of the Word and be accused of rejecting that same Word? How do you think you can avoid that accusation? Read Ezekiel 3:10 before you answer.

At the end of chapter 8, we catch a glimpse into Jeremiah's heart. How is he feeling about the situation? About His people? About their response to the message he gives? Do you have this kind of concern about your family? Your church? Your nation?

"Dear brothers and sisters, not many of you should become teachers in the church, for we who teach will be judged more strictly."

James 3:1

Poor Jeremiah. He is beside himself with grief. He does not simply observe the disobedience of his people. He is not just frustrated by their lack of response. He is not sorry that they will have to pay for their sin. Jeremiah cares so much for his people that he feels their oncoming destruction with the same intensity he would for the death of a close family member.

Jeremiah is "all in." He has held back no part of himself. He is one hundred percent committed to his people. Their failure hurts as much as if it were his own. He feels their pain intensely.

Sometimes I struggle with complacency. I see parts of the modern church reject the clear teaching of the Bible and feel overwhelmed. I look at my world, at the sin and selfishness of my nation and think there is no hope. Sometimes, when the gospel is rejected, I take it personally and retreat, choosing not to share the Good News with anyone. I have to make a conscious choice to care about the people I meet in grocery lines or fabric stores. I have to remember to pray for the folks on the freeway or those on the news. I must prod myself to pray for the struggling church. It takes effort. How are you doing? How does Jeremiah's concern for his people compare to your own?

Don't forget that Jeremiah's primary concern was with those who had entered into a covenant relationship with God. Today the church most closely reflects that audience. When you think about the sin struggles of the church—sexual sins, power issues, wars over worship preferences, pride, divisions, gossip, and accusations—how concerned are you about these issues? Have you considered these things from God's point of view? Do you grieve, as Jeremiah did, for the consequences of these sins?

APPLY Jeremiah 9 begins with a treatise of Jeremiah's emotions? What does he wish he could do? Have you ever felt like you were given an overwhelming task? When you feel overwhelmed, what are you tempted to do?

In Jeremiah 9:3–6, God speaks again about His people, this time mentioning a new complaint. What is it?

Why do you suppose truth is so important to God? (If you need help, consider these scriptures: John 3:19; 14:16–17; 16:13; and Romans 3:4.) As you answer this question, you might like to think about the danger of a misdiagnosis, mentioned in the story at the beginning of this lesson.

APPLY How are you doing when it comes to honesty? Would you like to make some changes? What one thing might you do to begin growing in the area of honesty?

In chapter 8, God complains that the leaders of Judah have offered a superficial treatment for the people's mortal (fatal) wound. In physical terms, this would be like putting a band-aid on a severed arm. The leaders of Judah have misdiagnosed the problems occurring in Jerusalem. The spiritual disease the people suffer will kill them, unless someone provides an accurate diagnosis and treatment.

In every medical consultation, the physician hopes to evaluate his patient's primary complaint, (for instance, a patient might come in complaining of nothing more complex than fatigue). Then, after taking a careful history, the doctor documents his physical findings (for instance, rash, swollen lymph glands, bruising, or elevated temperature). Lastly, the doctor might order lab reports or further testing in order to develop a diagnosis.

Once the diagnosis is determined, then the course of treatment is chosen; the more accurate the diagnosis, the more likely the treatment will be successful. In some cases, the cause of the disease can be determined—for instance,

HOW HONEST ARE WE?

In 2002, Rutgers' Management Education Center polled 4,500 high school students. They found that seventy-five percent of the students cheated repeatedly in their coursework. More than half of the students didn't believe that copying answers on tests constituted cheating. When questioned about the appropriateness of cheating, one student responded this way, "We students know that the fact is we are almost completely judged on our grades. They are so important that we will sacrifice our own integrity to make a good impression."

In a 2006 Associated Press poll of one thousand people, just over half reported that they believe that lying is never justified. About four in ten of the respondents stated that lying is okay in a number of circumstances. And over two-thirds of those polled reported that lying is acceptable to protect someone's feelings. Young people, aged 18–29, are most likely to justify lying.

Of those who confessed to a recent lie, fifty-one percent reported lying to a friend or family member.

CIRCUMCISION

For you are not a true Jew just because you were born of Jewish parents or because you have gone through the ceremony of circumcision. No, a true Jew is one whose heart is right with God. And true circumcision is not merely obeying the letter of the law; rather, it is a change of heart produced by God's Spirit. And a person with a changed heart seeks praise from God, not from people. (Romans 2:28–29)

exposure to contaminated water or exposure to an infected individual. This kind of information can help in diagnosis, and also prevent recurrent disease.

Most of us want to connect our illness with its origin. I've often watched as cancer patients struggle to understand what put them at risk. They are most baffled when nothing can explain their current illness. Nearly everyone knows someone who has contracted lung cancer without smoking a single cigarette.

Just as we desire to know and fully understand our medical diagnoses, Jesus, the Great Physician, wants His people to be aware of their spiritual diagnosis. We see this in the instructions He gives through Jeremiah. As we deal with our spiritual problems, God wants us to have an accurate diagnosis. Then, He wants us to understand where the disease came from. Only then—when we truly face what is wrong in our spiritual health—can we begin to turn to God for our healing.

In the paragraph beginning in Jeremiah 9:13, God gives the explanation for His people's inability to walk in truth. The scripture reads as if God is the "soul doctor," describing where the illness came from, how it developed and spread. His words include what a modern physician might call the prognosis—a prediction of how the disease will run its full course. According to this passage, name the primary reason that the people find themselves with a mortal wound?

____

____

APPLY If you want to avoid this kind of mortal wound in your own life, what things might you do, or promise, or seek after in order to avoid this same diagnosis?

____

____

____

According to Jeremiah, there is a strong relationship between falsehood and the mortal wound that threatens to kill his people. The people of Judah have adopted a lying lifestyle, one that neither values nor accepts truth. And along with that, they have lost their love for God. Verse 13 says, *"They care nothing for me."* It is a sad soul condition for Jeremiah's people.

We can struggle with the same disease. We can kid ourselves about our habits. We can deny the effects of watching questionable movies, spending too much time on the Internet, working too hard or too long, spending too much time volunteering (even for church), or not investing in the study of God's Word. And, as long as we deny the truth about our lives, as long as we turn away from the truth God gives us in His Word, we risk letting the disease process go on for so long that it becomes a mortal wound. A habit becomes a character trait, and before long we prefer the Internet to the Word, or work over church. Eventually the character trait becomes entrenched, and sin has room to take over.

Unless we remain open to the truth, keeping a diligent eye on our own commitment to truth, we—like Jeremiah's people—run the risk of becoming cold toward God.

Bringing It All Together

In Jeremiah 9:23 God tells three very different kinds of people that they should not boast. Who are they and what should they avoid boasting about?

Instead, if we boast, what should be our only source of pride (see 9:24)?

What do you think it means to "truly know" God? How does one go about that? How are you doing in your quest to know God? What might you do today to move forward, getting to know God more intimately?

After thirty-three years of marriage, I think I know my husband. I can sometimes finish his sentences. I know where he is going even before he finishes his thoughts. I know what makes him laugh. I know what makes him frustrated. I know his values and his passions.

I wish I knew God as well.

The older I get, the more I realize how little I know about God. It's true. When I was young, I had all the answers. I knew who God was, what He thought, what He would do in every situation. I had painted Him into a tight little corner, thinking that He would happily stay there. As I've grown older, I've begun to realize how very much I have to learn.

God is too big, too powerful, too wise for me to understand completely. In spite of this truth, I have committed the rest of my life to growing in my understanding of God. I try to stay close to Him, listening, learning, observing. I read His word with the hot passion of a mystery reader trying to figure out "who dunnit."

Knowing God is not a passive recreation. It involves prayer, thought, questions, and fellowship. Like mountain climbing, the path is difficult, but the view from the top is worth the trip.

In Jeremiah 9:26, God compares His own people to the people of the world. How are the two alike?

COLOSSIANS 1:9–10

So we have not stopped praying for you since we first heard about you. We ask God to give you complete knowledge of his will and to give you spiritual wisdom and understanding. Then the way you live will always honor and please the Lord, and your lives will produce every kind of good fruit. All the while, you will grow as you learn to know God better and better.

As I Follow God:

One summer, many years ago, our family headed north on a new-used powerboat. We motored all day, up through the Puget Sound to Port Townsend. Late that same afternoon, with one eye on the clock and the other on the weather, we decided to cross the Strait of Juan de Fuca, hoping to make Victoria, British Columbia (on Vancouver Island), before nightfall. Ahead, sunshine glimmered off calm water, and because the thirteen-mile crossing looked safe enough, we left land behind and headed across the straits.

An hour later, a heavy west wind and strong currents hit us on the port side of our boat. Waves battered us, sending salt spray over the windshield and onto our charts. We kept our speed up, watching the compass and fighting the weather. In spite of continued effort, we couldn't seem to make any real progress over the water. My husband suggested we start some serious praying.

Then, unexpectedly, the *Victoria Clipper*—a local tourist ship—crossed our bow (the front of our boat) from right to left. I asked Kim, "If the *Clipper* is going from Seattle to Victoria, why is it going across the bow from right to left? Shouldn't it pass us from behind?"

He laughed. "Maybe it's on the way to Alaska or something."

It just didn't make sense. As far as we knew, we were headed the right direction. We had the correct compass heading, the right charts; we'd continued progress in the right direction. What could have gone wrong?

Later, when I took my turn at the helm, I noticed a familiar shape in the distance. It can't be possible, I thought. But the closer we came, the more certain I was that we were not anywhere near Vancouver Island. In fact, the now recognizable land mass was the south end of San Juan Island, nearly twelve miles east of our destination.

In order to confirm our location, I checked the latitude and longitude of Victoria Harbor. Then, I checked our global positioning system. No question. We were off, but by how much? After some calculations, I realized that though our boat was "pointed" in the right direction, the wind and tide (pushing hard on the left side of the boat) had succeeded in pushing us steadily off course.

When I realized what had happened, I had a couple of choices: I could have decided that the global positioning unit was wrong and ignored it. Or, I could have decided that the chart was incorrect and continued looking for Victoria on the wrong island!

Or, I could change course.

Being the experienced skipper that I am, I called my husband up from the engine room! Then, after talking it over, we hung a sharp left turn. No matter how carefully we'd laid our course, something had gone seriously wrong. The only wise thing to do was to change direction.

Hours later, just as the sun sank in the western horizon, we motored into Victoria Harbor and tied up. At the end of a long day, both Kim and I were grateful that we'd discovered our mistake and taken steps to correct it.

CIRCUMCISION IN THE OLD TESTAMENT

Then God said to Abraham, "Your responsibility is to obey the terms of the covenant. You and all your descendants have this continual responsibility. This is the covenant that you and your descendants must keep: Each male among you must be circumcised. You must cut off the flesh of your foreskin as a sign of the covenant between me and you. From generation to generation, every male child must be circumcised on the eighth day after his birth. . . . All must be circumcised. Your bodies will bear the mark of my everlasting covenant. (Genesis 17:9–13)

The Jewish rite of circumcision was instituted by God through Abraham, and reinforced by Moses in the book of Leviticus. According to Jewish law, the foreskin of the male penis was to be removed on the eighth day after his birth. This part of Jewish life became central to their identity. Jacob's sons even went so far as to use this requirement to take advantage of their enemies, killing entire communities while the men recovered from their circumcisions (see Genesis 34:24–27).

The people of Judah experienced a similar predicament. Somehow, though they started off well, they'd managed to get off course. When God pointed this out, they faced a choice. They could continue on, ignoring the evidence of their mistake, or they could turn around.

In medical terms, the people of Jeremiah's time suffered from a fatal wound. They exhibited a complex collection of symptoms. They worshiped idols. They sacrificed their children. They were chronic liars. They were disobedient, unteachable, and proud of all the wrong things. They had closed ears and stubborn hearts. The citizens of Judah were deceived about their own spiritual condition, and frankly, they didn't want to correct their misconceptions.

Instead of changing course, they wanted Jeremiah to quit talking.

Fortunately for us, Jeremiah never gave up. Whether they listened or not, Jeremiah continued to speak in the city, at the entrance of the Temple and anywhere else the people gathered. Jeremiah continued to faithfully give God's message.

Obeying God, Jeremiah corrected, warned and taught the Judeans.

But God's people shut their ears.

When I think about this lesson, I consider how easy it is for us contemporary Christians to become enamored with our own journey. We get busy fighting the adversary, battling our circumstances, doing God's good work. And even while doing the best we can, sometimes we discover ourselves off course, deep in the sea of sin.

It happens to the best of us. An unhealthy relationship. A bad habit. A wounded heart. A reserved revenge. A neglected discipline. A secret fear. It happens to me.

But as far as possible, I want to be the kind of person who can—at any point in my life, whether public or private—make a course correction. I want to embrace repentance. To agree with God. To admit my disease. To seek treatment for my own fatal wound.

In the life of the soul, there is no wound more fatal than willful disobedience. And the only salve that heals is repentance. This is the way the soul changes course. Repentance is hanging a big left turn when you find yourself drifting away from God. Not only do we begin our spiritual life with repentance, but we also persist with repentance. In repentance we keep our life in Christ continually fresh. Continually alive.

No matter what sin entangles me, I hope that I always embrace repentance.

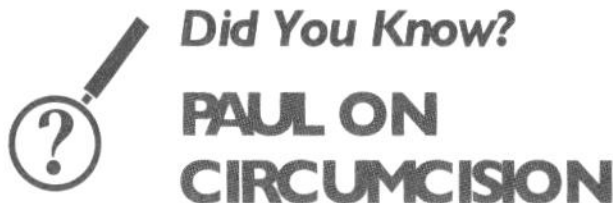

Did You Know?

PAUL ON CIRCUMCISION

While circumcision did not begin with the Jewish nation (the rite is also found in ancient Egyptian, African, Australian, and Aztec cultures), it became a symbol of Jewish spiritual and national superiority. Early on, Jews began to take pride in their circumcision, so much so that to them, it nearly became a talisman against threats from outside forces.

The intense emotion surrounding circumcision is still evident in the New Testament, where early Jewish converts sought to force new Gentile believers to adopt circumcision as a required ritual.

To this Paul answers, *"Watch out for those dogs, those wicked men and their evil deeds, those mutilators who say you must be circumcised to be saved. For we who worship God in the Spirit are the only ones who are truly circumcised. We put no confidence in human effort. Instead, we boast about what Christ has done for us"* (Philippians 3:1–3).

GOD SHAPES US

For our earthly fathers disciplined us for a few years, doing the best they knew how. But God's discipline is always good for us, so that we might share in his holiness. No discipline is enjoyable while it is happening—it's painful! But afterward there will be a peaceful harvest of right living for those who are trained in this way. (Hebrews 12:10–11)

Notes

lesson 4

Jeremiah 10–13

Clinging to God

I am married to a man of lists. With a type-A personality, and a massive collection of little pieces of paper, Kim manages to complete more in a single day than I can in a week. His lists litter the counters at our house; in fact, I found one on my desk this morning! Each one captures a glimpse into his step-by-step plan for accomplishing his many goals. While most people make lists of errands or chores, Kim even makes lists of individual subjects he wants to cover during personal telephone calls!

Kim is a man determined to finish his tasks.

With these qualities in mind, it shouldn't have surprised me when, as a young newlywed, Kim behaved as though he'd accomplished everything on his getting married list. Ask a girl out. Check. Determine if she's the ideal life partner. Check. Ask her to marry me. Check. Get married. Check. Go on honeymoon. Check.

Having accomplished the goal of finding himself a wife, Kim immediately moved onto the next item on his to-do list. In his case, it was dental school, and in those early years as a new bride, I felt abandoned and a little betrayed. I no longer made the list.

Fortunately, we've figured things out. With patience, we've learned not to take one another for granted. We try to invest in our relationship, spending time together, talking about our inner lives, turning away from the distractions of the world to make a deeper connection with one another. It hasn't always been easy.

Kim is a man determined to finish his tasks. . . . Having accomplished the goal of finding a wife, he immediately moved onto the next item on his to-do list.

Our situation is mirrored in many homes throughout our society. Men and women can be pretty goal-oriented people. They forget that a marriage isn't an accomplishment; it's a relationship requiring attention, work, and a constant investment of time.

A marital relationship is a living, breathing entity. When people treat it like an accomplishment on a to-do list, the relationship frequently dies. Even when the partners stay married, they often do so by rote. Marriage can become nothing more than obligation.

The same is true for our relationship with God.

We can be like the people of Jeremiah's audience, believing that our relationship with God begins and ends with our commitment to Him. Like a husband who signs his marriage license and then moves on, we can make a commitment to Christ and become absorbed by the details of life. We move on, thinking that God will take care of Himself.

This week's lesson focuses on the vital, life-giving relationship that each of us must have with God. We were meant to cling to Him, as a belt clings to the waist of the wearer. We'll face some tough questions this week.

What are you doing to cling to God?

Jeremiah 10–13

DAY ONE

" 'As a belt clings to a person's waist, so I created Judah and Israel to cling to me,' says the LORD. 'They were to be my people, my pride, my glory—an honor to my name. But they would not listen to me.' "

Jeremiah 13:11

A DIFFERENT PEOPLE

So far, our faithful Jeremiah hasn't made much progress. Though he continues to speak for God, the people refuse to listen. By now, if I were Jeremiah, I'd be frustrated enough to tell God to find another spokesman. Nothing makes me want to quit more easily than feeling unappreciated or ineffective.

After all, I don't have to suffer to be ineffective. I can be useless while sitting in front of the television set!

In this week's lesson, we'll discover that Jeremiah struggles with these same feelings. His heart is broken for his people. He wants them to recognize disaster on the horizon and change—not for his sake—but for their own. His patience with his ministry is wearing thin. His persistence is growing weak. Like all faithful ministers, Jeremiah must come back to God seeking something only God can give. Jeremiah needs a recharge, new energy, and a new desire to continue in ministry.

That encourages me. Leaders get tired. Teachers get worn out. Speakers feel unappreciated. Servants find their arms growing weak and their tempers growing short. It's normal. This week, we'll let Jeremiah teach us how to dig for encouragement in those difficult moments.

At the same time, we'll learn something about how God intends His people to survive in the world of ministry. Using a marvelous illustration, Jeremiah gives us a picture of our position in God. You'll discover that we aren't meant to tough it out or fight our way through. Instead, we were meant to live in relationship with God. To cling to him.

Enjoy your work this week, my friend. Be encouraged. You can find the strength you need to follow God! We'll be covering Jeremiah chapters 10 through 13 this week.

📖 Jeremiah 10 begins with a direct quote. You can tell that someone is being quoted by observing the quotation marks that begin in verse 2 and end the quote in verse 8. Who is speaking here? In your own words, what instruction does the speaker give?

___

___

___

In this quote, God describes a nation that tries to read its future in the stars. What two things does He tell his people to avoid? Refer to the sidebar on astrology. To whom do you think God refers when He speaks about astrological forecasting?

___

Early Babylonian observers discovered that the sun and moon, planets and stars moved through the skies in roughly the same path every year. By dividing the sky into twelve zones and naming each zone for a nearby constellation, the Babylonians invented what we call the Zodiac. Today's modern Zodiac names come from Greek translations of the original Babylonian words.

Do you know the difference between astronomy and astrology? Astronomy is the scientific study of the planets and stars. These students study galaxies both near and far, noting the motion of the planetary bodies and predicting the effects of these motions on other planets. Astronomers are the experts who tell us when we will next view Halley's comet.

Astrologers, on the other hand, use the planets and stars to predict the future of our lives here on earth. You could consider these people nothing more than fortunetellers, predicting the future via planets instead of tea leaves or tarot cards.

The Babylonians were both astronomers and astrologers. They studied the sky and also used the sky to predict their own future. God clearly warns His people not to be afraid of these Babylonian predictions.

📖 In Jeremiah 10:6, the prophet interrupts the flow of the text—almost as if he can hardly hold back his deep and heartfelt praise for the mighty God of Israel. In the space below, use Jeremiah 10:6–16 to make a list. Contrast Jeremiah's view of God with the idols of his people.

God	Idols

Based on what you have discovered while making this list, comment on Jeremiah's heart. How does he feel about God? What does his commitment look like? How do you think his understanding of God affects his ministry?

I hope that I may someday have Jeremiah's passion and deep understanding of God. In this passage, Jeremiah notes God's power in both creating and sustaining the universe. The prophet acknowledges God's greatness and uniqueness. He recognizes the tendency of foolish humans to seek false gods. And above all, Jeremiah describes the unmatched magnificence of a God who will tolerate nothing but His rightful place in the human heart.

When we hear from God again, in Jeremiah 10:17, what does God say? To whom is He speaking?

According to the book *Science in Ancient Mesopotamia* by Carol Moss, (London: Franklin Watts, 1988), the ancient Babylonians were patient sky watchers who kept daily diaries of the phases of the moon, the path of the sun, and the movements of the stars. They noted eclipses and used mathematics to predict future celestial motion. Because they believed these motions were signs from the gods, they also made predictions based on the sky.

Jeremiah speaks personally in Jeremiah 10:19. What do you think is Jeremiah's primary emotion? What causes this emotion? What is his prayer for himself?

Don't forget that Jeremiah is living in the midst of a societal meltdown. At this point in the narrative, the prophet has seen at least one (and perhaps two) of the Babylonian invasions. According to Daniel, the princes have been removed to Babylon by this time. We see this truth echoed in verse 20, where Jeremiah says, *"my children have been taken away."*

Often, we believers look at biblical heroes as superhuman. It's easy to think of Abraham as a courageous man without fear or attachment, of Moses as a mighty loner, of David as being the most godly and unfairly abused man who ever lived. But Scripture denies these myths. Nowhere in Scripture is this more clearly portrayed than in the book of Jeremiah. This man grieved for his people, experiencing great anguish over their faults and the punishment they suffered.

I believe that Jeremiah's deep understanding of God enabled him to continue in his difficult assignment. When things around the prophet seemed completely out of control, Jeremiah knew that a Mighty God held everything in His hands. He knew no idol could be more powerful than the God of Israel, and he understood that if the earth itself trembled at God's anger, no faithful human need ever fear the power of a nation—especially one foolish enough to serve worthless idols.

In the words that close chapter 10, Jeremiah expresses his complete trust in God. *"I know Lord,"* he says, *"that a person's life is not his own. No one is able to plan his own course. So correct me Lord, but please be gentle. Do not correct me in anger, for I would die"* (Jeremiah 10:23–24).

As you close today's study, consider Jeremiah's words. Have you come to the place where you realize that your life is not your own? Or, are you still trying to control your own future? Do you know God well enough to trust Him with the course of your life?

Confronting Disobedience

Jeremiah 10–13

DAY TWO

God speaks to Jeremiah again in Jeremiah 11:1–8. Summarize the message God wants Jeremiah to speak to the people in a single sentence.

____

____

____

In this passage, God reminds His people that there is a curse associated with disobedience. You'll find the source of this idea in Deuteronomy 27—28. In these chapters, God (through Moses) instructs the people to have six tribes stand on one mountain, the mountain of blessing, and six tribes stand on another mountain, the mountain of curses. The Levites then shout the blessings and the curses to all the people of Israel.

Read these chapters in Deuteronomy and pay special attention to 28:1–14 (the blessings) and 28:15–68 (the curses), and then fill in the chart below. Note the contrasts between the blessings and the curses. Keeping these details in mind, what single word captures the difference between the two columns?

IDOLS

Such stupidity and ignorance! Their eyes are closed, and they cannot see. Their minds are shut, and they cannot think. The person who made the idol never stops to reflect, "Why, it's just a block of wood! I burned half of it for heat and used it to bake my bread and roast my meat. How can the rest of it be a god? Should I bow down to worship a piece of wood?" The poor, deluded fool feeds on ashes. He trusts something that can't help him at all. Yet he cannot bring himself to ask, "Is this idol that I'm holding in my hand a lie?" (Isaiah 44:18–20)

Blessings	Curses

Isn't it interesting, that God gives His people a choice? Choose between a blessed life or a cursed life, He says. It's not much different today. A good parent gives his children the same kinds of choices. "You can do whatever you want," we encourage our children. "However, if you don't study, you won't pass the test. If you don't wake up on time, you'll be late for school, and you'll earn detention. If you don't eat your dinner, you'll be hungry at bedtime."

Like a good parent, God gives us a choice. "Obey me, and be blessed. Disobey and be cursed." God never forces His children. But the choice we make has clearly defined consequences. Obedience is clearly the best choice.

📖 In Jeremiah 11:9, God describes a conspiracy. Who is conspiring? What is the evidence of the conspiracy?

____

____

____

"And now, Israel, what does the Lord your God require of you? He requires you to fear him, to live according to his will, to love and worship him with all your heart and soul."

Deuteronomy 10:12

God's people have chosen to trust in idols rather than the living God. Their choice will bring calamity down on them, a disaster they won't be able to escape. When the disaster happens, how will the people respond?

____

____

____

It interests me that even after the disaster begins, God's people will make the decision to pray and offer incense to their idols (verse 12). How tragic that even the coming disaster will not turn them from their foolish ways.

It would be easy to judge these people. Though we've all seen idols—Buddhas and fetishes, totem poles and carved images—in gift stores, museums, and on guided tours, most of us would never set up an idol and begin praying. But even Christians can fall into the trap of idol worship, especially if you define idol worship as anything that steals your attention and devotion from God. Using that definition, even godly ambitions and ministries can become idols.

APPLY Using this simple definition, can you think of other things that might become more important to you than your relationship to God? What have you done to prevent idolatry from gaining a foothold in your life?

____

____

____

____

____

____

Perhaps we're not so different than Jeremiah's audience. It's fairly easy to allow things to take priority over our relationship with God. Our busy lives demand lots of energy and attention. We tend to live life putting out fires—attending to the urgent crises that pop up in our days. When things go wrong in your life, what do you tend to do? What is your first response? Is there a way that you could take your difficult situation to God first? What might that look like?

____

____

A New Threat

Jeremiah 10–13

DAY THREE

In the next section of chapter 11, the story takes a frightening turn. Look at Jeremiah 11:18–19. Here, God tells Jeremiah something personal, something very important. What is it? Who is behind this threat?

____

____

____

Looking back at Jeremiah 1, where does Jeremiah come from? Why might this new threat in chapter 11 represent a very personal disappointment for Jeremiah?

____

____

____

What did the men of Anathoth want Jeremiah to do? Did Jeremiah comply?

____

____

Using Jeremiah 11:20, what decision does Jeremiah make that might enable him to survive emotionally in the midst of this betrayal?

____

____

One of my students once made this observation about the betrayal Jeremiah faced: "This threat would not have hurt Jeremiah nearly as much if it had come from strangers. Instead, it came from family, from people he cared about and trusted." I thought her comment was particularly insightful. Anathoth, in the land of Benjamin, had been set aside for the priests when the Israelites took the Promised Land (Joshua 21:17). These men were Jeremiah's relatives, also priests, men dedicated to serving God.

We aren't surprised when strangers hurt us. We expect revenge and retaliation from those who hate us. But how do you recover when someone you love wants you dead? This kind of wound bleeds a long time.

I think most believers will experience this kind of betrayal over the course of a lifetime. Perhaps we won't face death, but we may face ugly rumors, misunderstandings, jealousy, and other nasty backlashes from those we trust. When this happens, remember Jeremiah. Remember that Jeremiah committed his cause to God.

Put Yourself in Their Shoes

THE PAIN OF BETRAYAL

We've all experienced it. There is no pain like the pain we feel when someone we love turns against us. King David knew it; he cried out to God while Absalom—his own son—tried to take the kingdom from him. You probably know what it is to find out that a confidant has shared your secrets with others. You know how it feels to discover someone is spreading lies about you. But have you ever realized that God feels betrayed when we fail to put our trust in Him? I find it fascinating that God has left His betrayal and Jeremiah's betrayal in the same chapter. Certainly we can identify with Jeremiah's feelings as others seek to kill him. Perhaps God wants to use those feelings to help us understand how much He longs to have us trust in Him alone.

As someone in my class said, "You cannot be betrayed by someone you don't care about." She is right. It is God's deep love for us that makes our turning to idols so very painful to Him.

Betrayal. Have you ever thought that your betrayal hurts God?

The prophet left the problem in God's hands. Certainly, we should defend ourselves where appropriate. We should communicate honestly with those who seek to betray us. When possible, we should seek to resolve these conflicts. But when resolution is not possible, we can, like Jeremiah choose to commit the problem to God.

In this way, we can let go of our desire to avenge ourselves. We can rid ourselves of unforgiveness and retaliation. Jeremiah was confident that God would take care of him. We can experience that same confidence.

In the opening paragraph of Jeremiah 12, the prophet comes before God with a big question. Paraphrase the question in the space provided below:

____

____

____

In obvious frustration, Jeremiah makes this request, *"Drag these people away like helpless sheep to be butchered!"* Why do you think he might feel this way?

____

____

Linen is planted in the spring, usually in April. With a short growing season, the flax plant usually blooms in July and is harvested in August. Because every part of the plant is used, the plant is pulled up by the roots and left to dry in the fields. There, moisture from precipitation serves to rot the outer fibers of the stock, which are then removed and used to make fiberboard. The long, fine, inner fibers are then spun into thread, which is wet-loomed into fabric.

(http://www.irishlinen.co.uk/whatislinen/)

When God responds in verse 5, He seems to ignore Jeremiah's question. Instead, He addresses something else. What is it? Why do you think God responds this way?

____

____

Clearly, our Jeremiah isn't superhuman. His own emotions sometimes overwhelm him. Such is the case in Jeremiah 12. Still, in the face of Jeremiah's question, I also hear his deep confidence that he has freedom to question God. Verse 1 says, "*LORD, you always bring me justice when I bring a case before you.*"

Jeremiah knows that he can ask freely.

Notice too, that God does not rebuke Jeremiah for asking an honest question. Though God chooses to address something else entirely, He is not threatened by an honest question. You can feel free to ask God honest questions. And after you ask, be still and listen.

Jeremiah wants to focus on other people. But God wants to focus on Jeremiah. It's almost as if God says, "You leave this one to me Jeremiah." And then, God implies that Jeremiah has bigger difficulties ahead. His response seems to say, *You have much more service ahead Jeremiah. Use this time to grow in strength, so that when the real trial comes, you will be able to flourish.*

God seems to use Jeremiah's difficulties with others to shape and strengthen the prophet for further use!

In the next verse, God warns Jeremiah of another threat; his own brothers have turned against him. How does God tell Jeremiah to cope?

____

____

You'll notice that God does not tell Jeremiah to forgive his brothers, or to turn the other cheek. He doesn't encourage Jeremiah to pray for his brothers. Instead, He tells Jeremiah that these brothers can't be trusted, no matter what they say. In light of the New Testament, do these instructions surprise you, coming from God? Why?

In all honesty, I have to admit that God's response to the threat surprised me. I am reminded of Jesus' Sermon on the Mount, telling people to turn the other cheek, to go the extra mile, to forgive in order to be forgiven.

In general, I assume that these comments mean that I must continue in relationship with people who have hurt me (but who have not changed), thus allowing the hurt to be repeated, over and over and over again. But God is no fool. He teaches that we must forgive, not for the sake of those who offend us, but for ourselves. By forgiving, we set ourselves free from the memory of the hurt, from the desire for revenge.

However, the issue facing Jeremiah was entirely different. The question was not of forgiveness, but of trust. Should Jeremiah trust the people who wanted to kill him? God's wise answer was, *"Do not trust them."* God knew these brothers had not changed, and perhaps He knew that they would never change. Jeremiah would put his life in danger if he were to continue in relationship with these men.

Of course eventually, Jeremiah would need to forgive the soul wound these men had inflicted on him. But he need not continue in a trust relationship with them.

An Object Lesson

Jeremiah 10–13

DAY FOUR

In Jeremiah 12:14 God mentions Israel's neighbors for the first time. What does God say they are trying to do? Will they suffer consequences?

In Jeremiah 12:15–16 God makes a promise to these neighboring nations. What condition is required for God to keep the promise?

In chapter 13, God instructs Jeremiah in a very practical way. What does God tell Jeremiah to purchase? Make note of the details in verse 2. What does Jeremiah do with his new acquisition?

Did You Know?

THE MIGHTY EUPHRATES

This formidable river, more than 1700 miles long, originates in the highlands of Turkey and flows into Iraq, where it runs roughly parallel to the Tigris River. The land between these two rivers constitutes ancient Mesopotamia (meaning "between two rivers" in Greek). Here the Babylonian and Assyrian cultures developed. In southern Iraq the two rivers join, becoming the Shatt al Arab, which flows into the Persian Gulf.

For Jeremiah, the nearest shore of the Euphrates is more than two hundred miles away. God asks him to make this trip twice for a total of more than eight hundred miles of walking through rough and hostile territory.

Why do you think it is important that Jeremiah wore the belt for a while before taking it to the river?

Later, Jeremiah gets another message from God. He is instructed to make a long trip to a distant location (note sidebar on Euphrates river). What is he to do with the linen belt?

God speaks to Jeremiah *"a long time afterward."* What does God ask of Jeremiah? What does Jeremiah discover at the river?

God frequently speaks in practical terms His people can understand. Here, he uses the belt as a picture, saying that His people have become like this rotting belt. He tells Jeremiah that He will rot away the pride of His people. Then, He lists three decisions His people have made that make them as useless as a rotten belt. What are the three decisions according to verse 10?

1. _____

2. _____

3. _____

From your favorite translation of the Bible, write out Jeremiah 13:11 here:

(You might want to consider memorizing this verse.)

APPLY

Now rewrite the same verse as if God were speaking it directly to you. Use your own name, and personal pronouns whenever appropriate. How does the verse feel when you see it written this way? Can you read it out loud to yourself?

As always, God gives Jeremiah's audience another opportunity. What single impedance might keep God's people from repentance (see Jeremiah 13:15)? How has pride interfered with your own repentance in the past?

A PICTURE OF BETRAYAL.

Jeremiah 10–13

DAY FIVE

In Jeremiah 13:18, God gives a message to the royal family. What does He ask them to do? What does this action signify?

In his message to the king and his family, why does God say the event will occur? (See 13:22)

Is it possible for these people to change their ways?

Do you recognize the source of our modern expression, "Can a leopard change his spots?" Originally, it appears as God's way of saying that these particular sinners will not give up their sinning ways. In Jeremiah 13:25, God says He has measured out the consequences of their sin because they have done what two things?

Note again how similar this is to our Key Verse in Lesson 2. This problem is God's primary complaint and is listed over and over again throughout the book. How was it described in chapter 2? How is it described in 13:25? Watch for this same truth expressed in other ways as we progress through our study.

In Jeremiah 13:27 God uses a new term to describe Judah's betrayal. What is the term? Why do you think that He chose that term?

____

____

I am told that not all contemporary believers view spiritual idolatry in the same way. Some believe that the term idolatry can only refer to literal acts of worship toward something that takes the place of God. Others view spiritual idolatry as a believer allowing anything (other than God) to capture whatever attention, affection, and energy which God himself deserves. Of these two camps, I confess that I tend toward the latter perspective.

When it comes to idolatry, I prefer to err on the conservative side. I would rather guard my heart and mind from anything that might take my sole focus away from my Father—and the lover of my soul.

In the electronic book, *How to Survive an Affair,* Dr. Frank Gunzburg quotes Kathy Brown (www.resourcebuilder.com):

> After many weeks of lying numb in bed, I tried to get my life back together, but this horrible combination of emotions kept coming up. At first I just felt rage: a kind of anger I have never felt before and pray to God I never feel again.
>
> Slowly the rage turned into hatred. I wanted to kill him. I mean I really wanted to kill him. . . . It scares me to talk about it even now. I had no idea I was capable of such feelings of violence.
>
> Eventually I realized these emotions were masking what I really felt deep down inside: betrayed, humiliated, and defeated. What's more, I felt very, very sad. I felt like someone had died, and in a sense, someone had. At the time, I felt like the life I had worked so hard for was dead. I was the one who had died. My rage and hate were like a shield against these softer emotions. My heart hurt so much I didn't even want to feel. The heart can really break you know. Mine has. I've felt it.

I used to think that God used the concept of "adultery"—that is, infidelity between married couples—to describe the idolatry of Judah because He believed it would help us to understand the seriousness of our sin. But as I've thought about it, I think there is more to the picture than that. Throughout the Old Testament, God uses the picture of marital infidelity to symbolize Israel's unfaithfulness to Him. (The Book of Hosea is a classic example of this symbolism.) Today, when we think of the ideal marriage relationship and how precious such a relationship can be, we can be assured that His love for us goes beyond the strongest marital love. This picture—of the betrayal of infidelity—shows not only the severity of the sin of idolatry and of God's deep and abiding love for us, but also the intense pain He feels when we turn away from Him. He is as intensely hurt as Kathy Brown was when her husband was unfaithful.

Interesting isn't it, that God describes Judah's betrayal toward Him in the same chapter that Jeremiah experiencs the betrayal of his family?

Interesting isn't it, that God describes Judah's betrayal toward Him in the same chapter that Jeremiah experiences the betrayal of his family? I think the two occupy the same chapter for a reason. God wants Jeremiah, who has also been betrayed, to identify with God's emotions over the betrayal of his people.

Most people who betray a loved one don't start out to do so. In her book, *Forgiving the Unforgivable: Marital Unfaithfulness,* Nancy Anderson describes her move toward betrayal with these words:

> I was full of self-doubt and couldn't believe how easily I'd been swept away by my feelings. I didn't plunge into sin—I drifted in, like floating on an air mattress and falling asleep only to wake up a half mile from the beach. I had to swim with all my strength to pull my heart back to shore. (You can read the entire article at: www.familylife.com)

The same is true about betraying God. We rarely set out to abandon Him. Instead we begin by taking tiny little steps, each taking us further off course. What can you do today to keep yourself on course?

As I Follow God:
Vicki and I shared a fairly new friendship. Our children attended the same Christian school, and we carpooled together. She and her husband John had been childhood sweethearts. They lived in a small house with three very active boys. Over the years of our friendship, I was always struck by the obvious adoration I saw in John's eyes when he looked at Vicki. Secretly, I envied being adored in this way.

Occasionally our children played together, swimming at our house, riding ATVs at hers. When she finally became a Christian, she hosted a Bible study in her home, which I taught. She took her discipleship very seriously; Vicki asked questions, read her Bible, and attended church. For several years, she did well.

Then, surprisingly, I noticed that she stopped returning my phone calls. She cancelled the Bible study. Time passed. And then, one morning in early summer, she called and asked if I could come and talk with her.

Vicki had begun a relationship with another man. As I listened, she poured out her grief. She surprised me by expressing deep dissatisfaction with her husband. Convinced that he no longer loved her, her new boyfriend's attention had formed an almost unbreakable bond between them.

I tried to speak to her about the effect this affair would have on her family. She seemed to listen. We prayed together, and I left her house that day, believing that she would speak with her husband about her struggle and the two of them would try to repair their marriage.

To my surprise, they did not. Vicki had no desire to restore the love relationship she shared with her husband. Though her husband tried, he could not convince her to give up the boyfriend. Divorce followed, leaving an entire family devastated.

As I think about adultery—the destruction of a covenant relationship by the betrayal of a spouse will always remember Vicki. In many ways, she and Judah were very much alike. Both let little things draw them away from their first love.

Both demonstrate a principle I firmly believe. While it is wise to put strong boundaries around your marriage, preventing adultery is more than following wise rules and restrictions. The best prevention is a strong marriage.

The same is true in your relationship with God. If you want to avoid idol worship—adultery—you must work toward growing more and more in love with God. Jeremiah 13:11 states: " *'As a belt clings to a person's waist, so I created Judah and Israel to cling to me,' says the* LORD."

Doctrine

BOUNDARY BUZZWORDS

Today, nearly everyone has heard something about boundaries. Psychologists use the term to describe the limits that define us. Boundaries tell others what we are or are not. What we like or don't like. What we will tolerate or not tolerate. Here are some of my own boundaries:

- I like Italian food.
- I love chocolate.
- I don't like rhubarb.
- I need my sleep.
- I choose not to drink alcohol.
- I am a writer.
- I deeply value honesty.
- My strongest spiritual gift: teacher.

Did you know that God has boundaries too? The Bible is full of passages that describe His limits. From these we know what pleases Him, what angers Him and what He will not tolerate. Here is a very short list of some of God's boundaries: See if you can add to the list:

- I am love.
- I am a jealous God.
- I will not share your affection with others.
- I am the vinedresser.
- I discipline those I love.
- I can remove your sin.
- I require that you live justly, love mercy, and walk humbly with me.
- Anyone who harms you, harms my most precious possessions. I will raise my hand to crush them.

As a seamstress and fiber artist, I find it fascinating that God uses linen in this illustration. Linen is treasured for its two strongest characteristics. Pound for pound, there is no natural fiber stronger than linen. This is because the fiber has a hollow core, making it very light. And, this same hollow core allows linen garments to wick moisture from the skin, making it highly valued in warm climates. Unlike modern, man-made fibers, linen does not dry quickly. Instead, the linen holds the dampness, creating a cooling effect not unlike that of a swamp cooler.

Ironically, the very qualities that make linen highly valued, also put it at risk. Unless linen is kept dry, it is vulnerable to attack by mildew. And when mildew attacks a garment, the fibers are weakened—destroying the very strength that makes the fiber so valuable.

If we are the belt illustrated in this Jeremiah passage, then our health—avoiding attack from the outside—depends on clinging to God. What does it mean to cling to the Lord? How does that look in real life?

For me, it means having many loving connections with other strong believers. Their love for the Lord kindles my own. His work in their lives, their answers to prayer, even watching as they tackle their difficulties with faith encourage me to a deeper trust.

Clinging to the Lord means making frequent opportunities for worship—both corporate and private. I can't explain it, but I am able to reach a level of intimacy in corporate worship that I rarely attain on my own. I also make opportunity for long periods of private worship. One of my friends frequently makes worship compilations, CDs, that I enjoy while driving in my car. When I ride my bicycle on trails, I listen to my iPod®. In those holy moments, I frequently hear the soft whisper of the lover of my soul.

Clinging to the Lord means time spent in God's Word. His spirit speaks to me there. He is more real, more tangible in the Word. When I get away from the Word, I begin to forget about His love for me. In 1979, after one of my strong Christian friends challenged me, I began a yearly program of reading the Bible all the way through. These days, I don't always make it—but I just continue reading over and over. I almost never miss a day in the Word. This part of my love relationship with God keeps me vital, healthy.

One more thing: When I'm feeling lost, as if I cannot reach God, or He is not listening, sometimes I read the Psalms out loud. I concentrate on the passages that describe God, like Psalms 49:12–14.

I have many friends who have established their own methods of keeping a vital love life with God. Ask around. See what your mature Christian friends are doing. Try things out. Copy. Eliminate. Do whatever you must. But keep your relationship with God fresh and alive.Your soul health depends on it.

In the Book of Revelation, Jesus speaks to the church at Ephesus, saying *"You don't love me or each other as you did at first!"* (Revelation 2:4). His advice to the church is to go back and *"work as you did at first."* Jesus is saying here, do the things you did then.

Think about your own first love—your first boyfriend or girlfriend. What did you do in those days? My husband and I spent as much time as we could together. We held hands. We took long walks. I listened while my love spoke.

Did You Know?

MORE ABOUT LINEN

Perhaps one of the oldest fabrics known to man, linen has been in production for many thousands of years. According to a lecture on the history of linen, by W. H. Webb (found at http://www.ulsterlinen.com) "In the British Museum, London, are pieces of mummy-linen 6,000 years old. Recently cuttings from these were microscopically examined and photographed at the Linen Industry Research Institute, Belfast, and were found to be as structurally perfect as linen made today."

A linen headdress found in the Nahal Hemar Cave in Israel dates from 8,500 years ago. Linen is twice as strong as cotton and three times stronger than wool. The fiber will hold twenty percent of its weight in water before it begins to feel damp.

I considered his wants more important than my own. I told everyone in my life about my new love.

Our first romantic love gives us a good picture of the way to maintain our love relationship with God.

What did you do when you first came to Christ? Did you tell everyone you knew what had happened to you? Did you spend time with other believers? Did you study the Word with fervor? Did you let yourself go in worship?

___

___

___

If you want to prevent spiritual adultery, re-commit yourself to your love for God. Do the things you did at first. If you will, you will likely never find yourself drawn away from God.

No matter what it takes, commit yourself to your first love. Don't let anything come between you and the Lord. Don't even allow the good things to distract you—like long seasons of raising young children, the early, tumultuous years of a career, or the birth of a ministry. All these good and important things can steal from God. When we boil life down to the really important things, nothing compares to the importance of loving God.

Nothing.

If you constantly protect and develop your love relationship with God, you will never experience Judah's correction.

We were meant to cling to Jesus, as a belt clings to the waist. Are you doing what you can do to cling to Jesus?

REMEMBERING GOD'S LOVE

Go, inspect the city of Jerusalem. Walk around and count the many towers. Take note of the fortified walls, and tour all the citadels, that you may describe them to future generations. For that is what God is like. He is our God forever and ever, and he will guide us until we die. (Psalms 49:12–14)

Notes

lesson 5

Jeremiah 14–21

The Cost of Serving God

Representing God among people has always been a rewarding yet dangerous business. This is nowhere more true than in modern China, where detentions, arrests, torture, and repeated beatings are everyday occurrences. Interrogations there are normally accompanied by the jarring shock of cattle prods and clubs. According to Voice of the Martyrs, trials happen secretly, without family members or witnesses present. Defendants rarely meet with their attorneys before the trial date. Unexplained deaths happen with alarming regularity to house church leaders imprisoned in jails all over China.

Representing God among people has always been a rewarding yet dangerous business. This is nowhere more true than in modern China.

The lucky ones are sentenced to "Re-education through labor" camps, some for months, others for sequential sentences adding up to many years.

On March 14, 2004, authorities arrested House Church leader, Gu Changrong, a fifty-four year old woman who had the temerity to share her faith with the Communist Party secretary in her village. As thanks for her effort, Mr. Yu Mingfu called the police and accused Gu of "poisoning Communist Party members" with her Christian message. Gu was arrested and sentenced to one year of "re-education through labor" in a camp known for the harsh treatment and torture of its prisoners. She was fortunate.

On June 18, 2004, Ms. Jiang Zongxiu was beaten to death while in prison. Authorities told her family that she had experienced heart failure, in spite of obvious bruising covering her body.

Pastor Cai Zhuohua, a house church leader was arrested along with his wife and several family members. They were detained in separate facilities. It was later learned that Pastor Cai was tortured by police using an electric cattle prod.

Changrong experienced the same difficulty as many of God's servants. When you bring God's message to people, not all will respond with an open heart. Modern Christians sometimes think these hostilities began in New Testament days, with Jesus' crucifixion, and continued with Stephen (who was stoned), James (killed under Aggripa's rule), Philip (who was crucified in Heliopolis), Matthew (who was martyred by sword in Ethiopia), and James (Jesus' brother, who was stoned).

But the truth is, all through the Old Testament, God's people have suffered when they shared His message with the world. As far back as the book of Genesis we can observe people's rejection of God's message. In the story of Noah, of Lot, of Joseph, of Caleb, and Joshua, people have chosen to laugh at God's message for them. In the best of circumstances, the message is rejected. In the worst, the messenger himself—like Jesus and hundreds of China's house church leaders today—finds himself at the wrong end of a cattle prod. In this week's lesson, our friend Jeremiah is about to learn this same painful truth:

It isn't easy to be God's messenger.

Jeremiah 14–21

DAY ONE

TENSIONS INCREASE

In this lesson, you'll see that things have begun to change for the prophet Jeremiah. If this were a work of fiction, I would say that we are approaching the climax of the story. The conflict between Jeremiah and his audience continues to escalate. Like water in a teapot, things have begun to boil.

"Your words are what sustain me. They bring me great joy and are my heart's delight, for I bear your name, O LORD God Almighty."

Jeremiah 15:16

This week, you'll observe as Jeremiah's audience changes as well. The people's hearts are becoming harder and more resistant to God's message. Not only do they ignore Jeremiah's message, they begin to reject the messenger. They spread rumors about him and eventually decide to eliminate him all together.

At the same time, we see that God demands more and more of the faithful prophet. As his audience turns away from God and the tension increases, Jeremiah finds himself squeezed. The increasing pressure serves to forge Jeremiah's character, like steel plunged from fire to cold water. The process makes Jeremiah stronger.

Since we are not able to study every verse and phrase of Jeremiah, we'll have to choose carefully which passages we will study. If you can make time, try to read chapters 14 through 21 in a single sitting. Feel free to make notes in your Bible. Underline. Highlight. Then, come back and begin to answer these rather simple observation questions:

As the people turned away from God, even the land and the animals suffered consequences. You'll find it described in Jeremiah 14:1. What is happening?

When the people complain about their situation (14:7–9), what does the Lord reply?

In Jeremiah 14:7, God's people seem to be making an effort to repent. They acknowledge their sins. They remind God of His power to save. And yet, God does not rescue them. Why not? His response gives some hint of His reasoning. *"You love to wander far from me,"* he says in verse 10.

It seems that these people want God to "understand their sin." After all, they say, their *"backslidings are many"* (in the King James Version). It's almost like a gambling addict who says, "After all, I'm an addict, what do you expect? Just lend me a little more money!"

Though the people agree with God, they express no desire to turn away from their sin. For this reason, God rejects their appeal for help.

What do the prophets tell the people (14:13)?

What does God say that He will do to these prophets (Jeremiah 14:15)?

APPLY Even today, courageous people continue to speak for God. Not everyone couches these expressions with, "Thus saith the Lord." In what ways have you experienced humans who claim to have a message from the Lord?

Has this passage changed the way you feel about those who give false messages?

The prophet closes chapter 14 with a prayer. On what basis does Jeremiah appeal to the Lord for help?

Notice that Jeremiah's knowledge of God (remember the chart you made early in chapter 4?) comes into play as Jeremiah prays. The prophet knows enough about God to understand what might persuade God to listen. As Jeremiah prays, he reminds God of His promises to His people, of His reputation and of His mighty power. Not a bad way to pray!

JEREMIAH WEEPS

I weep for the hurt of my people. I am stunned and silent, mute with grief. Is there no medicine in Gilead? Is there no physician there? Why is there no healing for the wounds of my people? Oh that my eyes were a fountain of tears; I would weep forever! I would sob day and night for all my people who have been slaughtered. (Jeremiah 8:21—9:1)

PAUL WEEPS

In the presence of Christ, I speak with utter truthfulness—I do not lie—and my conscience and the Holy Spirit confirm that what I am saying is true. My heart is filled with bitter sorrow and unending grief for my people, my Jewish brothers and sisters. I would be willing to be forever cursed—cut off from Christ!—if that would save them. (Romans 9:1–3)

God Speaks to the Prophet

In chapter 15, we read the personal side of this dramatic story. The Lord speaks to Jeremiah in Jeremiah 15:1. At first glance, the entire chapter reads harshly. Why do you think that God would not listen to the supplications of Moses or Samuel for these people?

As you read verses 1–6, what single phrase expresses God's emotions about the current situation?

PSALM 22

My God, my God, why have you abandoned me? Why are you so far away when I groan for help? Every day I call to you, my God, but you do not answer. Every night you hear my voice, but I find no relief. But I am a worm and not a man. I am scorned and despised by all! Everyone who sees me mocks me. They sneer and shake their heads, saying, "Is this the one who relies on the Lord? Then let the Lord save him! If the Lord loves him so much, let the Lord rescue him!" (Psalm 22:1–2, 6–8)

Anyone who has ever lived with an addict understands God's feelings about his people. As the addict cycles through addiction, repentance, abstinence, and then falls back into addictive behavior, the people of Judah are cycling as well. Like the wife of an alcoholic, God has become weary with Judah's cycle (see verse 6). He will bring an end to it with the coming destruction of Jerusalem.

In Jeremiah 15:10–16 Jeremiah begins to express his own feelings in the midst of these troubles. What has happened to him in his community? How is he feeling? What does he ask God to do?

Even though Jeremiah is struggling, he expresses his delight in God's word. *"Your words are what sustain me,"* he says. *"They are my great joy."* Oh that we would all feel that way about God's word! How might that change the way we endure hardship?

Jeremiah asks God (15:18), *"Why does my suffering continue? Why is my wound so incurable? Your help seems as uncertain as a seasonal brook. It is like a spring that has gone dry."* It appears that Jeremiah has begun to doubt God, to resent God's work in his own life, as well as the life of his country. To this, God replies rather harshly in verse 19. Why do you think this infraction is so important to God? How might this kind of doubt disqualify us from speaking for God?

In Jeremiah 15:19, God says to Jeremiah, *"If you return to me, I will restore you so you can continue to serve me."* Why do you think Jeremiah must return? How has Jeremiah turned away from God? Can you find other words in the chapter that hint of his error?

Below, using a separate line for each, list the promises God makes to Jeremiah (Jeremiah 15:19–21). Underline these promises in your Bible. Use a red pen, if you have one. Keep these promises in mind as we progress through the study.

We'll look back to this question in future studies. But for now, I'd like you to keep the following verbs in mind:

Restore. Secure. Protect. Deliver. Rescue. Keep.

These are the verbs used in the New Living Translation for Jeremiah 15:20–21. (Though your translation may use different words, the meaning remains the same. Remember, verbs are action words!) Who is the person doing these action words? Jeremiah? God?

____

____

As this remarkable account continues, you will find God keeps His promises. By the end of the book, He will have done each of these things for Jeremiah. Mark your Bible as these actions occur.

THE PAIN OF MINISTRY

We are pressed on every side by troubles, but we are not crushed. We are perplexed, but not driven to despair. We are hunted down, but never abandoned by God. We get knocked down, but we are not destroyed. Through suffering, our bodies continue to share in the death of Jesus so that the life of Jesus may also be seen in our bodies.

Yes, we live under constant danger of death because we serve Jesus, so that the life of Jesus will be evident in our dying bodies. So we live in the face of death, but this has resulted in eternal life for you. (2 Corinthians 4:8–12)

The Difficulty of Service

Jeremiah 14–21

DAY THREE

In chapter 16, God imposes some restrictions on Jeremiah. List them here:

____

____

____

📖 Once again, God mentions His key complaint against the people. In chapter 2, he tells the people that they had forsaken Him, the fountain of living water, and dug cisterns that could hold no water. In Jeremiah 16:11 God repeats the charge again, using another phrase. What is it?

____

In the midst of God's accusations against the people, God takes a moment to offer hope. In the paragraph starting in 16:14, what promise does God make to His people?

This promise is important. Eventually, in chapter 21, we will see that God instructs the citizens of Jerusalem to surrender to Nebuchadnezzar and accept the coming deportation to Babylon. Imagine how much easier it might be to obey that order, when you know that God Himself has promised to bring you back!

In Jeremiah 17:5, God uses a word picture. Once again, He restates His main charge against the people. *"Cursed are those who put their trust in mere humans and turn their hearts away from the LORD."* The word picture that follows includes stark contrasts. What is contrasted, and very briefly, what does each represent?

PSALM 1:1–3

Oh, the joys of those who do not follow the advice of the wicked, or stand around with sinners or join in with mockers. But they delight in the law of the Lord, meditating on it day and night. They are like trees planted along the riverbank, bearing fruit each season. Their leaves never wither, and they prosper in all they do.

What are the qualities of people who trust in the Lord, and have made the Lord their hope and confidence? (See verses 7–8.)

In the word picture, what might the riverbank represent? What might the months of drought represent? What is the ultimate sign of the tree's enduring health?

Note that according to this passage, difficult seasons are a fact of life—even for the tree planted by Living Water. The New International Version translates Jeremiah 17:8 as *"when the heat comes"* (emphasis added), not "if the heat comes." Certainly we will all face dry seasons and tough times. But our relationship with God will, if we sink our roots deep into him, keep us alive, growing, and fruitful. That is a meaningful promise that I find very comforting.

According to Jeremiah 17:9, what is the condition of the human heart? Do humans have the ability to judge the heart? Who does? According to this passage, what is an important part of God's job description? Are you aware of a time when your own heart has deceived you?

Jeremiah 17:9 is a key text, supported by many, many other biblical passages. Contemporary society wants us to believe that all humans are basically good; only evil circumstances, poverty, or poor upbringing can turn us into murderers and thieves. When you believe that circumstances make humans evil, you will spend all of your resources trying to change those circumstances.

But the Bible disagrees. Humans suffer from a common illness. Jeremiah calls it heart disease. This is why we believers put all our resources into helping humans experience a change of heart. A heart transplant if you will.

Paul calls it our sin nature. *"I know I am rotten through and through so far as my old sinful nature is concerned. No matter which way I turn, I can't make myself do right. I want to, but I can't"* (Romans 7:18). Our wicked hearts have led us to sin.

Whenever we consider the human heart, we must remember that we are naturally wicked. Our motives are unclear—even to ourselves. Only by allowing God to inspect our deepest motives and inward desires can we ever hope to untangle the confusion that is bound up in the human heart. He searches all and knows us intimately. We can trust Him to untangle the confusion of the human heart.

📖 Beginning in 17:14, Jeremiah complains to God about those who are not receiving his message. What do these people say?

____

____

📖 Beginning in verse 16 the prophet speaks to God. *"I have been faithful,"* Jeremiah insists. What does he celebrate about God? Next, he makes a request of God. What is the request?

____

____

____

Our beloved prophet is human. We know from the last chapter that Jeremiah has committed the correction of his persecutors to God. But his fully human heart is hoping that God will do something about those who make his life miserable! *"Bring shame and terror on all who persecute me,"* he says. While God doesn't evaluate Jeremiah's attitude here, neither does he hide the true feelings of our friend the prophet.

God responds by giving Jeremiah another message. Where is he to go? What does God request? What new accusation appears in this passage? (See verses 19–23.)

____

____

____

____

APPLY For your consideration: Why do you think the Lord asked His people to maintain a Sabbath? What would the observance of a Sabbath day represent in a person's life? Why might it be important? Did you know that the Ten Commandments mandate a Sabbath day observance? Do you keep a Sabbath? Why or Why not? How?

____

____

____

____

____

We know that keeping the Sabbath appears as Commandment Number 4 in Exodus 20. God's people were expected to obey these commandments. This sin was more evidence that they had lost their fear of God. One by one, they had begun to disregard God's commands.

THE SABBATH

Observe the Sabbath day by keeping it holy, as the Lord your God has commanded you. You have six days each week for your ordinary work, but the seventh day is a Sabbath day of rest dedicated to the Lord your God. On that day no one in your household may do any work. This includes you, your sons and daughters, your male and female servants, your oxen and donkeys and other livestock, and any foreigners living among you. All your male and female servants must rest as you do. Remember that you were once slaves in Egypt, but the Lord your God brought you out with his strong hand and powerful arm. That is why the Lord your God has commanded you to rest on the Sabbath day. (Deuteronomy 5:12–15)

WHILE AT THE POTTER'S HOUSE

Jeremiah 18 opens with God's instruction to Jeremiah, *"Go down to the shop where clay pots and jars are made. I will speak to you while you are there."* What does Jeremiah observe at the potter's house?

___

___

What is the message that this picture demonstrates? What did God say about it?

___

___

___

Ultimately, God's sovereign hand is at work in all our decisions, yet He holds us responsible for the choices we make.

In doctrinal terms, Christians have long debated the issue of predetermination—the idea that God has predetermined every detail of our lives before we are born, even our response to the gospel. A rigid interpretation of this doctrine seems to make people nothing more than puppets in God's hands. Yet a more moderate view of this doctrine acknowledges the truth that God knows ahead of time what choices you and I will make—even before we make them. Ultimately, God's sovereign hand is at work in all our decisions, yet He holds us responsible for the choices we make.

The book of Jeremiah brings this question to the forefront. Readers might wonder, did God determine that His people would reject him? Did they ever really have a choice in the matter? Did God plan for the Babylonians to punish His people? And if He planned it, why does He then (Jeremiah 51:11–12) punish Babylon for carrying out His will?

Many of us struggle with these difficult questions: How much of my future does God determine ahead of time? And, if God has planned every detail of my life long in advance, then what difference do my choices really make? Do I really have any choice at all?

God's plan. Our response. Two interrelated forces that cannot be easily dissected.

It's easy to get lost in these kinds of discussions—something like wondering which came first, the chicken or the egg? We can twist ourselves into a knot trying to figure it all out. Some truths about God are difficult to understand, and Jeremiah has just bumped into one of these truths. In Jeremiah 18:5–11 God clearly says that He will respond to our choices. If we choose repentance, He will decide to forgo our correction and instead bless us. If we choose rebellion, He will forgo our blessing and decide instead to correct us.

We see this truth shown clearly in many Old Testament stories. Clearly God has foreknowledge and a divine plan; but He also responds to our choices. This is just one example of the tension we must accept when we follow a God who is beyond our understanding. Because He responds to our choices, we know that we must choose wisely.

📖 What choice do the people make in 18:12?

Not only do these people refuse to listen, but they begin to attack Jeremiah personally. What campaign do they wage against him in 18:18?

📖 Read verses 19–23. How is Jeremiah feeling about his audience? What does he ask God to do?

Perhaps the most insidious of weapons, rumors, are still widely used in today's wars. I've known pastors who find themselves battling an enemy with no shape, no source, no reality. Rumors flourish among people. They disqualify the messenger and free the guilty from repentance. God's people used rumors to destroy Jeremiah's reputation.

While Jeremiah's audience used rumors with evil intentions, today we sometimes find ourselves inadvertently sucked into similar situations. Keep yourself from participating in the war of rumor and speculation.

📖 In Jeremiah 19:10–13, God asks the prophet to go buy a clay jar. What is he instructed to do with the jar? What is the meaning of this object lesson?

What new sin does God bring to focus beginning in 19:4? God determines that at least one consequence will happen as a result of this sin. What is the consequence? What does the severity of this consequence imply about God's values?

Many writers have compared this child sacrifice to the modern sin of abortion. In this analogy, sexual promiscuity has become the idol of our modern age; unwanted pregnancy becomes the stimulus for child sacrifice. It's a frightening analogy, but certainly worth considering. Yet we must remember that our job in this study is not to condemn our culture. Of course many behave with ungodly values. But let us turn the light of examination on ourselves. I know it may be difficult, even convicting, but can you think of another way that modern Christians might be sacrificing their children on an altar to a foreign god?

PAUL PAYS THE PRICE

Then some Jews arrived from Antioch and Iconium and won the crowds to their side. They stoned Paul and dragged him out of town, thinking he was dead. But as the believers gathered around him, he got up and went back into the town. The next day he left with Barnabas for Derbe. (Acts 14:19–20)

Did You Know?

THE TRAGEDY OF ABORTION

According to the Alan Guttmacher Institute (an affiliate of Planned Parenthood), from 1973 through 2002, more than 42 million legal abortions occurred in the United States. Approximately 1.4 million elective abortions happen every year. Of those, about half occur in women who have already had at least one abortion (www.guttmacher.org).

JEREMIAH FACES ARREST

Jeremiah 20 begins with a new problem. The priest in charge of the Temple decides to take matters into his own hands. What does he do to Jeremiah? How long does the event last?

____

____

____

📖 When Jeremiah is released, he gives Pashhur a personal prophecy (20:3–6). What does he promise will happen?

____

____

Until now, Jeremiah has suffered through psychological abuse. He's been threatened; people have promised murder and spread vicious rumors about him. But this is the first recorded physical abuse given to the prophet. Why do you think this is an escalation of trouble against Jeremiah?

____

____

____

In 20:7–9, the prophet lets us see his personal anguish. He states that he is mocked, that his name is a household joke. More than that, his old friends seem to be waiting for him to slip up. They hope he will speak so that they can report him to the king. Even his friends want revenge.

Part of Jeremiah wants to give up. . . . Part of him wishes he had not been born. Still Jeremiah repeats his trust in God in verses 11 and 12 of chapter 20.

Part of Jeremiah wants to give up. *"My entire life has been trouble, sorrow, and shame."* Part of him wishes he had not been born.

Still, Jeremiah repeats his trust in God. *"They cannot defeat me,"* he says. Once again, he commits his cause to God. *"Let me see your vengeance against them, for I have committed my cause to you"* (verse 12). We'll look at this declaration more closely later.

📖 Even as ministry takes its toll, Jeremiah faces a personal struggle as well—something my father used to express as "darned if you do and darned if you don't." What form does this contemporary proverb take in Jeremiah's life (see verses 8–9)?

____

____

____

What burns like a fire in Jeremiah's bones?

____

📖 Read the paragraph which begins with Jeremiah's declaration in 20:11. How has Jeremiah changed compared to his declaration in 15:17? Why do you think he has changed?

Jeremiah is no superhuman. He faces the same struggles that we do. He doesn't like to be rejected, or made fun of. In fact, at this point in his life, Jeremiah could not see that he had made a single difference in the lives of those around him. He ends chapter 20 with a wish that he had never been born.

APPLY Have you ever felt that your life makes no difference to anyone? When? In retrospect, has your perspective changed? How?

Chapter 21 gives an account of a frightening confrontation. Who comes to see Jeremiah, and what is their request? Does this seem ironic to you? Why?

God tells the king (through Jeremiah) that He will not grant the king's request. In fact, God is going to ensure that Jewish weapons will be useless against the Babylonian army. God tells king Zedekiah that He is going to send a terrible plague upon the city, and when death has run its course, God will hand the city over to the Babylonians (21:3–10). At this point, the message takes a new turn. What new instruction does God gives the people? What choice do they face?

In our culture, surrender is unacceptable.

In our culture, surrender is unacceptable. There is hardly an American citizen who cannot quote Patrick Henry's famous phrase, "Give me liberty, or give me death!" But there is a point in every believer's life where surrender is surely the wisest course.

Surrender means to give up. To change course.

When God makes His direction clear and we choose to go another way, surrender is the best decision we can make. When sin has taken root in our heart, and we have repeatedly given in to its pleasure, surrender to God is the best course. When we surrender to the Holy Spirit—to our own inability to overcome—to the truth of our own nature, then we are empowered to live a new life. By agreeing with God, we access God's power for change; only then can we leave the old behavior behind, and live the victory that He intended.

In spite of Patrick Henry's famous proclamation, for believers, surrender is often our first and finest choice.

As I Follow God:
I commend you, my friend. You've made it through a long and difficult lesson this week. You've found answers, considered applications, and thought about ways the truth has surfaced in your own life. You've worked hard.

Most people who undertake a study like this one already have a deep commitment to the Lord. They want to follow him, but more than that, they want their lives to count.

I know I do.

And I want to be able to represent the Lord in my community, whether the community of believers or the wider community where I live. I want to bring Him honor, to speak the truth with a love so profound that others are stilled by what they hear.

I want to live a holy life, though there are days I think that this is the most impossible of dreams. I cringe to think that my actions, my temper, or even my off-the-cuff comments might somehow keep someone from knowing the God I love so deeply.

I want to speak for God—to speak words that move people toward God, that inspire, that encourage, that teach. And when I think of this deep longing that I hide in my heart, I think of Jeremiah.

Speaking for God cost Jeremiah.

He sacrificed marriage, family, festivities, weddings, even relationships with the people who knew him best. God asked Jeremiah to forgo these things, not because they were bad, but because these sacrifices enabled Jeremiah to better serve God.

God had given Jeremiah a gift, the gift of speaking for God. Jeremiah simply received the gift and put it to good use.

Please note. Jeremiah didn't beg God for a job and then earn it by sacrificing the things he loved best. This would be akin to asceticism—earning relationship or position with God by living a life of poverty and sacrifice. Instead, Jeremiah simply experienced relationship. God had given Jeremiah a gift, the gift of speaking for Him. Jeremiah simply received the gift and put it to good use.

In the context of this relationship, God asked for more from Jeremiah. And Jeremiah said, "Yes."

All through the centuries, many of God's servants have paid the high cost of ministry. Though the details differ, personal sacrifices cost God's people dearly.

For some, God said, "Leave your family."
For others he said, "You may not marry."
For some, "Leave your country."
For some, he says, "Give up that hobby." Or, "Take this position, though you will never afford your own home."

Recently, friends of ours retired from running a successful Tacoma business. Rather than travel or rest and enjoy the remainder of their lives, God asked Tom and Kathy to begin a new adventure. They have bought a large home in Africa where they host short-term missionaries, visitors, and donors for a local orphanage. God asked Tom and Kathy to do more. He asked them to give up their retirement plans.

In contemporary terms, I think of Billy Graham, who spent very little time at home during his children's early years. Or Brother Yun, of China's Underground Church, who spent only seven of his first twenty-one years of marriage actually living with his wife. Instead, he lived in hiding, preaching the gospel, suffering in prisons, and starting new churches. I think of Hudson Taylor, whose harsh missionary life cost him the lives of five children and two wives. In spite of the difficulty, Taylor served China for fifty-one years, making eleven trips between England and China.

These men and women didn't initiate the sacrifice. They responded to it. They loved God and longed to serve Him; compared to serving God, nothing else mattered.

If you want to speak for God, you must expect to hear Him whisper in your ear. You must be willing to put everything on the table, your time, your hobbies, your dreams, your ambitions, your social connections—everything—so that you can live the productive life He has for you.

Are you listening? Will you lay it down?

Notes

lesson 6

Jeremiah 22–37

When Bad News Is Good News

When her mother called late in the week of November 9, 1970, to tell her that her father had fallen ill, Lucy Kautz knew that she would have to change her weekend plans. She would never think of leaving her mother in need. Still, Lucy couldn't help feeling disappointed. Her husband, the university's athletic director, would have to go on to the football game without her.

The game promised to be a good one. In spite of a losing season, their team showed steady improvement. The players were coming together, working hard, and showing the kind of winning spirit that might finally turn things around. Though the school had narrowly avoided being removed from the Southern Conference after facing NCAA restrictions for recruiting violations, everyone agreed it was only a matter of time before they achieved a winning season. At last, it seemed like luck might have finally begun to break their way.

In spite of her disappointment, Lucy kissed her husband goodbye and stayed at home. On Saturday evening, after a long day with her father, she went shopping with her youngest daughter. "I was in such a hurry to get home. Over and over, I said to her, 'You've got to hurry. Your dad is going to be home any moment.' On the way home, I was too harried to listen to the radio. But when I drove into the driveway, and saw all those people at the house, I knew. I knew even before I went inside."

Lucy went shopping with her youngest daughter. "I was in such a hurry to get home. Over and over, I said to her, '. . . Your dad is going to be home any moment.' On the way home, I was too harried to listen to the radio. But when I drove into the driveway, and saw all those people at the house, I knew . . . even before I went inside.

On November 14, 1970, at 7 PM, after a flight of less than an hour, the plane carrying her husband Charles Kautz and thirty-seven Marshall University football players, eight coaches, twenty-five community members, and a flight crew of five had crashed as it approached the runway. There were no survivors. In the fiery aftermath, many bodies were burned beyond recognition. The crash devastated both the community of Huntington, West Virginia, and the Marshall campus community as well. It would be years before the grief gave way.

For Lucy Kautz, what seemed like bad news—her father's illness—became the very event that saved her life. Though she would forever grieve for her husband Charles, at least she had not left her children as orphans, stripped of both parents in the same fateful event. Having lived through the weekend, Lucy found herself caught in the emotional turmoil of survivor's guilt. At least she was alive.

This week, we'll watch Jeremiah go through a similar experience. What seems to be a tragic turn of events becomes his saving grace. Can you learn Jeremiah's lesson? Can you begin to see the good news in bad news?

Jeremiah 22–37

DAY ONE

Reviewing Jeremiah's Experience

This week, we'll look at chapters 22–37 of Jeremiah. Don't panic! It won't be nearly as difficult as you imagine! If you have time, try to read these chapters in one or two sittings.

JEREMIAH 37:21

So King Zedekiah commanded that Jeremiah not be returned to the dungeon. Instead, he was imprisoned in the courtyard of the guard in the royal palace. The king also commanded that Jeremiah be given a loaf of fresh bread every day as long as there was any left in the city. So Jeremiah was put in the palace prison.

With fifty-two chapters, the Book of Jeremiah is one of the longer books in the Bible. Because we can't read and comment on every chapter and verse in only eight weeks, we'll use this week to take an overview of Jeremiah's life through the next fifteen chapters. We'll cover a lot of territory without going into tremendous detail.

Your goal should be simple. Try to get a feel for Jeremiah's struggles, for the responses of the people, the other prophets, the priests and the king. As you read these chapters, remember that God's evidence against the people continues to mount. In chapter 21, Nebuchadnezzar is already at the city gates; the famine has begun, and the drought has intensified.

As the clouds of disaster darken with every chapter, I have to wonder how the people continue to believe that Jeremiah was lying. As they resist, watch how God adjusts His message. If you pay attention, you will learn much about God's ways with His people.

At the same time, put yourself in Jeremiah's place. Feel the discouragement of his endless battle against a stubborn and unrepentant people. Feel his fear as a campaign mounts to end his ministry, in fact, to end his life.

I must warn you of something that may confuse you. The chapters we'll study this week do not appear in chronological order. In chapter 21, the message sent to Jeremiah is from Zedekiah, the last king of Judah before the city was completely destroyed. But, in chapter 22, Jeremiah records a message given to Jehoiakim, who actually reigned *before* King Zedekiah. To help you place these messages, refer often to the chart, **"The Last Kings of Judah,"** found on page 142. This will help you keep track of these sometimes confusing events.

Lets begin this week's study!

📖 In Jeremiah 22:1, Jeremiah confronts someone with great power. Who is it? What is the message? For whom is the message given?

____

____

____

📖 Look at Jeremiah 22:13–17. Is this part of the message to King Jehoiakim personal or does it refer to the behavior of the nation? What is the message? What part of Jehoiakim's character is addressed here?

____

____

____

____

📖 In Jeremiah 22:21, God mentions Jehoiakim's childhood. What is the issue? What might this verse say about the importance of establishing God's reign in your children's hearts?

____

____

____

It seems that Jehoiakim has a longstanding problem. Even as a boy, he refused to listen to God's instruction. While we don't know anything specific about his childhood, God does. And God tells us that He has warned this king earlier regarding his character.

As parents, I read in this message both good and bad news. It reminds me of the importance of teaching my children to willingly submit to God's authority. Because this lesson is easiest to learn in our early years, I must press on!

On the other hand, this story tells me that God—the perfect parent—shows longsuffering while teaching Jehoiakim about obedience. Jehoiakim, in his stubbornness, obviously didn't learn much. We all have known some children so deeply embedded in rebellion that we wonder if God Himself can drive it out. Perhaps before you became a Christian, you were considered by some to be a "lost cause."

Jehoiakim has given himself over to greed, and greed is a dangerous taskmaster. Greed will get under your skin. It will make you treat people like possessions. It will allow you to use and oppress others. It will pervert your sense of justice and fairness. It will give you a stiff neck and deaf ears. James 4:1–2 gives us the same message:

> *What is causing the quarrels and fights among you? Isn't it the whole army of evil desires at war within you? You want what you don't have, so you scheme and kill to get it. You are jealous for what others have, and you can't possess it, so you fight and quarrel to take it away from them.*

JOSIAH'S REPENTANCE

When the king heard what was written in the Book of the Law, he tore his clothes in despair. Then he gave these orders to Hilkiah the priest, Ahikam son of Shaphan, Acbor son of Micaiah, Shaphan the court secretary, and Asaiah the king's personal adviser: "Go to the Temple and speak to the Lord for me and for the people and for all Judah. Inquire about the words written in this scroll that has been found. For the Lord's great anger is burning against us because our ancestors have not obeyed the words in this scroll. We have not been doing everything it says we must do. (2 Kings 22:11–13)

MORE ON JOSIAH

The king took his place of authority beside the pillar and renewed the covenant in the Lord's presence. He pledged to obey the Lord by keeping all his commands, laws, and decrees with all his heart and soul. In this way, he confirmed all the terms of the covenant that were written in the scroll, and all the people pledged themselves to the covenant. (2 Kings 23:3)

Jehoiakim has chosen a life characterized by self-centered greed. And God cares enough to warn him about the consequences of his choice.

📖 In 23:1–4, God gives Jeremiah a message about a specific group of people. Who are they? What is their sin?

____

____

____

Do you think that God is speaking about the shepherds who care for furry farm animals? Why or why not? Who are they? Compare this to Matthew 18:12. What is God's will for His sheep?

____

____

____

This theme—the importance of faithful leadership— recurs throughout the Old and New Testaments. In Ezekiel (see sidebar), God rebukes leaders who have used and abused His people. In the book of Luke, Jesus chastises the leaders of His day with these words, *". . . how terrible it will be for you. For you crush people beneath impossible religious demands and you never lift a finger to help ease the burden"* (Luke 11:46). James warns teachers that God will judge them with greater strictness. Paul tells Timothy (the pastor at Ephesus) to keep a close watch on his own life and his teaching so that he would be beyond reproach.

God wants leaders who care for His people, lovingly leading them toward repentance and obedience. He will not tolerate leaders who profess one thing and live another. Knowing this, we who consider ourselves leaders should, like Timothy, lead circumspect lives, willing at all times to respond to correction by the Holy Spirit.

📖 An important passage is found in Jeremiah 23:5. To whom do you think this passage refers? You might want to read Isaiah 11:1–5.

____

I don't know why, but I am still startled in Old Testament passages, when suddenly, seemingly out of nowhere, God reminds us of His promise to send the Messiah. In this particular passage, God's message through Jeremiah focuses on Jesus the King, who will rule with wisdom. His name, "The LORD is our Righteousness," comes from the Hebrew word *Tsidqenu.* In this one phrase—though even Jeremiah himself may not have understood— we catch a glimmer of Jesus' divine and future work on the cross. Through His death, we have our righteousness. Through His payment for sin, our sin is forgiven. Through His resurrection, we are forever deemed righteous in God's sight.

You might be surprised to see how passages from Old Testament books add up to a detailed profile of the promised Messiah. Some Bible scholars estimate that Jesus' life fulfilled more than three hundred prophetic verses. In studies like this one, you can begin to see the miracle of those passages, most written hundreds of years before Christ, as they are fulfilled in Jesus' life and ministry.

What glory, what joy we find in this tiny reference, ensconced in a rebuke for an unrighteous leader. It seems as if God cannot keep His plan a secret. Here, He reminds us that a perfect leader is yet to come!

EZEKIEL AND THE SHEPHERDS OF ISRAEL

Then this message came to me from the Lord: "Son of man, prophesy against the shepherds, the leaders of Israel. Give them this message from the Sovereign Lord: What sorrow awaits you shepherds who feed yourselves instead of your flocks. Shouldn't shepherds feed their sheep? You drink the milk, wear the wool, and butcher the best animals, but you let your flocks starve. You have not taken care of the weak. You have not tended the sick or bound up the injured. You have not gone looking for those who have wandered away and are lost. Instead, you have ruled them with harshness and cruelty. So my sheep have been scattered without a shepherd, and they are easy prey for any wild animal. They have wandered through all the mountains and all the hills, across the face of the earth, yet no one has gone to search for them. (Ezekiel 34:1–6)

"Never before had there been a king like Josiah, who turned to the Lord with all his heart and soul and strength, obeying all the laws of Moses. And there has never been a king like him since."

2 Kings 23:25

In a related passage, beginning in Jeremiah 23:9, God speaks about the false prophets. Will these men go unpunished? What will happen to them? Looking at Jeremiah 23:18, 22, what one thing might these men have done to hear from God?

What does this tell you about their desire to hear God?

APPLY Listening to God might be both an art and a skill. Think about your own life. Would you say you are growing in listening to God? How?

Jeremiah's Message Evolves

Jeremiah 22–37
DAY TWO

In Jeremiah 24:3, God gives Jeremiah a vision of two bowls of figs. In this vision one bowl contains fresh ripe figs, while the other contains figs that are too rotten to eat. In your own words, what do the two bowls represent? (Look at the entire 24:3–10 passage.)

In this passage, we read the first real details about God's plan for His people who go into exile. I don't think the people in Jerusalem believed that God might bless them in exile. After all, they thought, wouldn't exile be outside of God's perfect will for them? Yet, God gives them another message. Here He makes it plain that He will bless those in exile, giving them good treatment and a promise to return to their own land and to God, wholeheartedly.

As chapter 25 opens, in verse 3 Jeremiah tells us how long he has been preaching. How many years has he been faithfully serving God?

Have the people responded to his message?

Think how that must have felt—preaching for more than two decades without any apparent change in your audience. In fact, if anything, Jeremiah's audience has become more hard-hearted. More stiff-necked. Is your character strong enough to faithfully follow your assignment for this many years without experiencing any results? Does this make you re-think your frustration with your own ministry over the years?

In 25:12, God tells Jeremiah something about the captivity still to come. How long will the captivity last? What will happen to the Babylonians when it is over?

In Daniel 9:2 we read, *"I Daniel was studying the writings of the prophets, I learned from the word of the LORD, as recorded by Jeremiah the prophet, that Jerusalem must lie desolate for seventy years."* Isn't it amazing to see that Jeremiah's message became a source of hope for Daniel—who at the time of this writing was already an old man serving in the kingdom of Persia?

In the passage beginning in Jeremiah 25:9, God's words take on a more specific warning. God no longer uses general terms about an enemy from the north (as He does in the first chapters of Jeremiah). Now, He warns that He will *"gather all the armies of the north under King Nebuchadnezzar of Babylon. . . . I will bring them all against this land and its people and against the other nations near you. I will completely destroy you and make you an object of horror and contempt and a ruin forever."*

In chapter 26, Jeremiah is asked to go stand in front of the Temple and speak to the people. His message—turn from evil and follow God—remains the same. How do the people, priests, and prophets respond (Jeremiah 26:8)? How has their response intensified?

APPLY Do you think continued rebellion generally produces this outcome? In other words, do you believe that stubborn hearts frequently become more and more hateful toward truth-tellers? How have you observed this in your own faith journey?

After the first deportation of people from Jerusalem (which included Daniel and his three friends), Jeremiah's message has changed in a very significant way. Instead of "repent, and this disaster can be avoided," what does he tell the people in 27:17?

Note also the new message of hope (now being repeated over and over) found in the last words of chapter 27. In the space below, write down the key factor that should give them hope.

In chapter 28, another prophet—a false prophet—gives a message that directly contradicts Jeremiah's. Who is it, and what does he say?

In Jeremiah 28:15, Jeremiah gives Hananiah God's response. What does God say? In the space below, note what happens to the false prophet:

____

____

____

I probably shouldn't, but I feel a little sorry for Hananiah. After all, who wouldn't want to believe that God would defeat the Babylonians? This false prophet had watched as his people began the inescapable slide into the mouth of the Babylonian dynasty. Of course he wanted God to defend them. The only problem is that Hananiah began to believe his own press release. And no matter how much he hoped for deliverance, he had no business sharing his hope as God's prophetic word.

Notice that Jeremiah does not allow himself to be caught up in the battle between prophets. He does not defend his own message. Instead, he simply reminds Hananiah that every prophet bears the burden of proof. Hananiah's prophetic word would be proven only if the words come true.

When Hananiah personally attacks Jeremiah, breaking the yoke on his neck, and declaring a new and different outcome for the people of Jerusalem, Jeremiah does not respond. He simply leaves the Temple area. He walks away. In doing so, Jeremiah shows us his great self-control, modeling for us the wisdom of letting God fight our battles with those who devalue or dispute our ministry.

Put Yourself in Their Shoes

ONE MAN'S COURAGE

Poor Jeremiah! Though he had faithfully served God, he suddenly found himself facing a court who would decide whether or not to turn him over to an angry mob. Chapter 26 ends with this key verse, *"Ahikam, son of Shaphan also stood with Jeremiah and persuaded the court not to turn him over to the mob to be killed."*

Only one man, unknown and unsung, had the courage to stand with Jeremiah against them all—prophets, priests, authorities and many others. And that one man managed to turn the tide of the court toward Jeremiah. His intervention saved Jeremiah's life. Would you have had the courage to take that action?

Working with Prophecy

Jeremiah 22–37

DAY THREE

In Jeremiah 29, the prophet writes a letter to those already exiled in Babylon. Read this letter carefully. (It begins in verse 4.) This passage contains a frequently quoted and deeply loved Old Testament verse. (You'll find it written out in the sidebar for you.) Considering the **context** of the passage, make an argument for why this passage should **not** be globally applied to all Christians everywhere. Then, for the strength of argument, explain how this passage might indeed apply to all believers.

Why this passage is not applicable to all believers:

____

____

____

____

____

____

Why this passage applies to all believers:

____

____

____

JEREMIAH 29:11–14

"For I know the plans I have for you," says the Lord. "They are plans for good and not for disaster, to give you a future and a hope. In those days when you pray, I will listen. If you look for me in earnest, you will find me when you seek me. I will be found by you," says the Lord.

I hope this exercise hasn't discouraged you from taking God's promises as your own. My goal is for you to see the difference between a biblical promise as it pertained to the people for whom it was written, and that same promise as it might apply to us several thousand years later.

The context here is very important isn't it?

In verse 11, Jeremiah writes, " *'For I know the plans I have for you,' says the* LORD, *'They are plans for good and not for disaster, to give you a future and a hope.'* "

In the context of the Book of Jeremiah, these plans apply to God's blueprint for restoring His desperately wicked and rebellious people. God wants to use this punishment in Babylon to change His people, to cleanse them of their wickedness, to bring them back into their land a humble and repentant people. So, perhaps we modern readers should only consider this scripture as a promise for us when we too are in the midst of God's loving discipline. Also, the text clearly implies a condition of repentance. " *'If you look for me in earnest, you will find me when you seek me. I will be found by you,' says the* LORD."

Considering the context or environment of this passage, I doubt that it means that we can blatantly go along on our own way and claim God's good plans for us. Rather, this passage is best applied to the suffering believer who has willingly submitted to God's loving discipline. In that case, no matter what we face, we can know with confidence that God has our best in mind.

JEREMIAH 30:12–17

"This is what the Lord says: yours is an incurable bruise, a terrible wound. There is no one to help you or bind up your injury. You are beyond the help of any medicine. All your allies have left you and do not care about you anymore. I have wounded you cruelly, as though I were your enemy. For your sins are many and your guilt is great. Why do you protest your punishment—this wound that has no cure? I have had to punish you because your sins are many and your guilt is great. "But in that coming day, all who destroy you will be destroyed, and all your enemies will be sent into exile. Those who plunder you will be plundered, and those who attack you will be attacked. I will give you back your health and heal your wounds, says the Lord.

Whenever we choose to appropriate a passage as a promise in our own life, we must carefully consider the people for whom the passage was originally intended. And we must never get more out of the passage than God intends for us to receive.

📖 In 30:2 the Lord gives Jeremiah a new task. What is it? What specifically does God seem to have in mind for this task?

Note especially 30:18. God says that Jerusalem will be rebuilt on her ruins and that the palace will be reconstructed as it was before. Verse 21 says something quite remarkable—that Israel will have its own ruler again and this ruler will not be a foreigner. According to history, no Jewish king ever ruled Israel autonomously again. (For instance, we know that King Herod served as a puppet of the Roman Empire.) In addition to this mysterious ruler, God says, *"You will be my people, and I will be your God."* These conditions don't seem to have been fulfilled after the captivity. To whom might this passage refer?

An especially important passage appears in Jeremiah 31:31–34. What event does God predict here. How will this new covenant be different from the old one?

Note the amazing promise found in 31:38–40. Thinking historically, has this promise been fulfilled? Why do you think so?

Prophetic scripture can be confusing—even to those carefully schooled in biblical interpretation. You can sometimes clear up your own questions simply by observing each passage very carefully. The details included can eliminate many possible interpretations and applications. As you look at this kind of scripture, it helps to remember that sections of prophecy may actually refer to two or more different events. The details about those separate events may appear within the same paragraph, or sometimes, even within the same verse.

For instance, some Bible scholars believe that passages referring to Judah's return to the land of Israel pertain both to the return of Jews after the captivity and at the same time to the return of Jews after World War II—when the modern nation of Israel was created.

I've heard this concept, the concept of double meaning, explained this way:

When you look at prophetic scripture, imagine that you are looking at a panoramic photograph of a mountain range. In this kind of photo, the mountains appear to lie in a straight line off in the distance. In truth, some of those mountains are much closer to the viewer than others. The same is true of prophetic scripture. While all of the words appear to refer to some distant event, in fact, parts of the prophecy may refer to events of imminent fulfillment, while other parts of the same passage may refer to a more distant event—perhaps even to events yet to be fulfilled.

Rather than be confused by these things, I consider it a treasure hunt. I look for passages that might have more than one fulfillment. I scour the scriptures for passages that may refer to the coming of Messiah (Jesus), or to His second return, or even to Jesus' final reign, after all things are completed.

To increase my accuracy with these passages, I try to make sure that every interpretation is supported by prophetic revelation found in other biblical passages. This concept helps us to link prophetic books—like Isaiah, Daniel, Ezekiel, and Revelation. By putting these passages together, we can sometimes fill in the details of the events yet to come.

Remember that prophetic Scripture is rarely crystal clear. Many prophetic experts lived at the time of Jesus' ministry. However, these same experts did not recognize Jesus as the Messiah. Is it possible that they failed to identify Him because they were so absolutely certain that they knew exactly what the messianic prophetic scriptures meant? Were they so distracted by what they believed the scriptures meant that they forgot what the scriptures actually said?

We are called to recognize prophetic fulfillment **when** it occurs rather than spend all our energy guessing about its meaning and timing **before** it occurs.

JEREMIAH 31:35–37

It is the Lord who provides the sun to light the day and the moon and stars to light the night, and who stirs the sea into roaring waves. His name is the Lord of Heaven's Armies, and this is what he says: "I am as likely to reject my people Israel as I am to abolish the laws of nature!"

This is what the Lord says: "Just as the heavens cannot be measured and the foundations of the earth cannot be explored, so I will not consider casting them away for the evil they have done. I, the Lord, have spoken!

Be careful not to elevate any one person's interpretation of prophecy to the level of biblical truth. We protect ourselves from that error by focusing on the actual content of Scripture rather than its interpretation.

If we carefully examine the scriptures, knowing exactly what these passages say, we will be far less likely to be fooled into accepting any one person's portrait of how Scripture will be fulfilled; at the same time, we will have all the tools we need to recognize its fulfillment as it occurs.

Jeremiah 22–37

DAY FOUR

CORRECTION AND REDEMPTION

In chapter 32, Jeremiah's life has taken a turn for the worse. Look at Jeremiah 32:1–5. What has happened to the city?

____

____

What has happened to Jeremiah?

____

____

JEREMIAH 33:24–26

"Have you heard what people are saying?—'The Lord chose Judah and Israel and then abandoned them!' They are sneering and saying that Israel is not worthy to be counted as a nation. But this is the LORD's reply: I would no more reject my people than I would change my laws of night and day, of earth and sky. I will never abandon the descendants of Jacob or David, my servant, or change the plan that David's descendants will rule the descendants of Abraham, Isaac, and Jacob. Instead, I will restore them to their land and have mercy on them."

A large portion of Jeremiah 32 concerns the purchase of land. If you read carefully, the actual event may have occurred not after Jeremiah was imprisoned, but while he was giving the forbidden prophecy. At any rate, Jeremiah's cousin Hanamel from Anathoth (Jeremiah's home town) offers a piece of family land to Jeremiah. God tells Jeremiah to return home and pay the required price to buy the land.

God uses this simple purchase as a picture to remind Jeremiah's audience that a time will come when the people will again buy and sell land. The Jews will not be gone from the land forever. They will return. They will take up their family lands and resume their lives in Israel.

In chapter 32, God paints a dramatic contrast to the events beginning to happen around them. The city walls are surrounded by siege ramps. Jerusalem has been closed off, with no food entering the city. Drought, famine and disease are rampant; on the outside things look very grim. In the midst of this, God gives both the picture of restoration and the reality of imminent destruction. God leaves these two messages side by side. Punishment and redemption. Both together, side by side.

I wonder, are these things contrasted because compared to their impending doom, the redemption appears that much sweeter? Or is it because during the siege the people might give up hope? Or is it that God longs to have His people recognize His grace in the midst of their own rebellion?

____

____

____

Only God can answer. As for me, I love the sweet flavor of redemption placed alongside the bitter pill of punishment. Whenever they appear together, I am overwhelmed by the grace and goodness of God.

In chapter 34, Jeremiah gives a message to King Zedekiah. Jeremiah promises that Nebuchadnezzar will capture the city and lead Zedekiah to Babylon, where he will live out his days. Note the passage in Jeremiah 34:22:

> *And though Babylon's king has left this city for a while, I* (God) *will call the Babylonian armies back again. They will fight against this city and will capture and burn it.*

This unusual note is explained further in Jeremiah 37:5:

> *At this time, the army of Pharaoh Hophra of Egypt appeared at the southern border of Judah. When the Babylonian army heard about it, they withdrew from their siege of Jerusalem.*

In chapter 35, God uses another picture to speak to his people. Here, Jeremiah commends a group of Recabites, saying, *"The Recabites do not drink wine because their ancestor Jehonadab told them not to."* These people were obedient to their ancestors' instructions—though they were nothing more than ordinary people. In contrast, God's people refuse to obey Him, though their laws came from God Himself.

In chapter 36, we see additional evidence that parts of Jeremiah do not appear in chronological order. King Zedekiah (the central character of chapter 34) actually took office after King Jehoiakim (the central character of chapter 36).

Let's pause and make some observations in chapter 36: In verse 1, God instructs Jeremiah to write down every message he has been given. What is God's hope for this exercise? How is His purpose here different than His purpose in chapter 30 (Jeremiah 30:1–3)?

____

____

____

Who actually did the writing for Jeremiah?

____

What is Jeremiah's condition at the time of the writing (36:5)?

____

What does Jeremiah ask Baruch to do?

____

____

Interestingly, God twice asks Jeremiah to write down the messages He has given the prophet. The first time, it seems that God wants the messages documented so that as they are fulfilled, God's prophetic accuracy would be confirmed. However the second time, God wants His people to have yet another opportunity to repent.

How faithful is our God! How diligent He is, chasing us to the very corner of our world, determined that we would chose His way over our own.

Did You Know?

ZEDEKIAH'S FOLLY

When Nebuchadnezzar crowned Zedekiah king, the new king of Judah signed an oath that he would not betray or revolt against Babylon. However, in the ninth year of his reign, Zedekiah made a secret alliance with Pharaoh of Egypt. Nebuchadnezzar caught wind of Zedekiah's betrayal, and headed immediately for Jerusalem, where he began a siege against the city. Egypt somehow heard about the attack on her ally and started out to defend Jerusalem. It was this approaching Egyptian army that temporarily distracted Nebuchadnezzar from his attack on Jerusalem. After soundly defeating Egypt, Nebuchadnezzar returned and continued the attack on Judah and Jerusalem. In only eighteen short months, Nebuchadnezzar breached Jerusalem's walls, entering to destroy the city, burn the Temple and take down the walls surrounding her.

As Baruch reads the scroll in the Temple, one member of the audience takes a message to the palace. The palace secretaries then ask Baruch to come and read the scroll to them. The words of Jeremiah badly frighten these men. What do they instruct Jeremiah and Baruch to do?

____

PAUL'S IMPRISONMENT

And I want you to know, dear brothers and sisters, that everything that has happened to me here has helped to spread the Good News. For everyone here, including all the soldiers in the palace guard, knows that I am in chains because of Christ. And because of my imprisonment, many of the Christians here have gained confidence and become more bold in telling others about Christ. (Philippians 1:12–15)

Would these guards have known about Jesus without Paul's imprisonment?

When King Jehoiakim finally hears the words of the scroll what does he do? What do you think this action symbolizes?

____

____

Isn't it interesting how the same words have two very different effects on these men? Some tremble in fear, understanding the cost of disobeying God. Others scorn God, using the event as an opportunity to display their arrogant rebellion against the King of the Universe. God's Word continues to bring out our truest self, revealing our inner motives and core character.

After listening to the words of the scroll, the king gives orders to arrest Jeremiah and Baruch. What simple line explains what happens next (36:26)? Don't you wish you might have watched that part of the story unfold?

____

____

____

In complete disregard for the Word of God, King Jehoiakim burns the scroll that Jeremiah has dictated. When Jeremiah re-wrote the scroll, was it the same?

____

Jeremiah 22–37

DAY FIVE

FROM BAD TO PRISON

Congratulations, my friend. You've covered a lot of ground this week. I admire your tenacity. Certainly during this study you've found moments to pause and thank God for His amazing kindness in preserving this record. You have undoubtedly rejoiced in His promise of a redeemer, fulfilled in Jesus. Take heart. You're almost finished. Take a deep breath and plunge forward. We'll take only a brief look at chapter 37.

Once again, we see that the chronology of chapter 37 does not follow chapter 36. The first paragraph of chapter 37 tells us that Zedekiah is king, and that Jeremiah had not yet been imprisoned. So mentally we must move forward and even a bit backward in time. Remember that by the time this passage begins, King Nebuchadnezzar had begun the siege on the city but had gone away to face Egypt's Pharaoh in battle.

As this chapter opens, God describes the attitude of the people this way, *"Neither King Zedekiah nor his officials nor the people who were left in the land listened to what the LORD said through Jeremiah."* A sad state of affairs. May no one ever say that of us.

What does Zedekiah ask of Jeremiah?

What words does Jeremiah share with the king?

Jeremiah does not have any encouragement to give the king. Instead, the prophet tells the king that the destruction of the city has been determined. The Babylonians would return from battling Egypt and burn Jerusalem to the ground.

After this confrontation, because the siege has been temporarily lifted, Jeremiah tries to go out and visit the land he bought in Anathoth. What happens to him? What are the accusations against him?

When Jeremiah is imprisoned in a dungeon cell, the king calls for him secretly (Jeremiah 37:17). What is the king's request? What is Jeremiah's response?

Jeremiah bravely makes another request. What is it?

What happens to Jeremiah in the final paragraph of chapter 37?

As I Follow God:
I've ended this week's long study at one of my favorite little notations in scripture. Our hero, Jeremiah, finds himself in prison. How demoralized he must have felt. How tempted he must have been to blame God. "You could have stopped this," he might have whined. "I've served you faithfully. Why am I in prison? I'm the only one in this city who is really listening to you. What kind of reward is this for my faithful service?"

Maybe Jeremiah was more mature than this. We'll never know. I only know that I'd be tempted to let bitterness creep in. I'd wonder what good it did to obey God. In the process, I might manage to lose sight of this most important fact:

In a city of starving citizens, Jeremiah was put in a place where he had a loaf of bread every single day—as long as any bread was left in the city.

What looked like abandonment may actually have been God's supernatural

JOHN'S EXILE

I was exiled to the island of Patmos for preaching the word of God and for my testimony about Jesus. It was the Lord's Day, and I was worshiping in the Spirit. Suddenly, I heard behind me a loud voice like a trumpet blast. It said, "Write in a book everything you see, and send it to the seven churches in the cities of Ephesus, Smyrna, Pergamum, Thyatira, Sardis, Philadelphia, and Laodicea." (Revelation 1:9b–11)

provision for the faithful prophet. While God didn't remove him from the circumstances in Jerusalem, God made sure that Jeremiah didn't starve. In prison, he was safe from those who wanted him dead. He was provided bread when everyone else was starving.

Perhaps you don't know, but this famine grew so severe that women ate their own dead children—children who had succumbed to starvation and dehydration because of the siege. (Lamentations 5:10 says, *"Tenderhearted women have cooked their own children and eaten them in order to survive the siege."*)

At the time, did Jeremiah have the foresight to see his predicament in the light of God's kindness? I doubt it. Yet all through church history, we hear story after story of what appears to be disaster—which in retrospect is nothing more than God's grace disguised. I think of Paul's imprisonment in Rome, which gave him time to write most of the New Testament. I remember the persecution of the Church, detailed early in the book of Acts, which sent believers running from Jerusalem. Because of the danger, Scripture reports,

> *A great wave of persecution began that day, sweeping over the church in Jerusalem, and all the believers except the apostles fled into Judea and Samaria.* (Acts 8:1)

Without that persecution, it might have taken those early believers decades to bring the Good News of Jesus to a desperate world. Would they have become complacent and comfortable in Jerusalem? Would they have been happy to "play church" rather than share Christ? Perhaps. Thank goodness we'll never know!

One of the benefits of a long life in Christ is the joy of looking back at some of life's difficult events from the perspective of God's grace and provision. When my husband graduated from dental school in 1979, we planned to move to a tiny town in eastern Washington. Though we had almost no money and few earthly possessions, we'd carefully budgeted for the move, purchased used dental equipment, rented a house and—because we had no maternity coverage with our medical insurance—saved for the birth of our first child. As we schemed and planned and saved, we had complete confidence that we would soon be earning a salary.

To our dismay, the baby did not come on time. We waited three long weeks for Eric's birth. Each week, the doctor exhorted me to have patience. At one appointment he suggested I start a knitting project to help me pass the time. "What kind of project," I asked. "A potholder, or a sweater?"

To our dismay, all our plans fell through. The dentist, who hosted my husband during his third summer in dental school, decided that he would not share his office space. Suddenly we had nowhere to go and no resources to carry us through until we could open our own practice. I remember that late spring evening when the news came through; both my husband and I spent the gloaming hours crying on our couch. Why had this happened? We believed we'd been listening to God. How could we have gone so wrong?

Even now, I'm not certain that I understand all the details. I can say this; God provided desperately needed funds by effecting a change in my health insurance—completely unknown to us. Effective May 1 of that year, maternity benefits, which had previously been excluded, began to be covered as part of our major medical coverage. Because the baby came late, just days after our health insurance changed, Eric's birth was completely covered as a major medical expense! For months we were able to live off the money we'd scrimped and saved to pay the hospital.

Though we'd planned to live in eastern Washington, we started a dental practice in a fast-growing Puget Sound community. Kim's business did well, and our rural community exploded into a suburb of Seattle.

Then, twelve years after starting our practice in Puyallup, Washington, God called us to help plant a church. Starting a church from scratch is the hardest thing I've ever done. Yet, it has been by far the most rewarding! In the process, I've discovered in myself both a teacher and a writer. I've written and directed drama, played worship piano, taught Bible studies, and edited newsletters. I doubt we'd ever have experienced such a rewarding challenge in the tiny town where we'd planned to go.

Somewhere in the pain of that false start, God miraculously boosted our faith, provided for our finances and redirected our path. Now, nearly thirty years later, I can see God's grace in the experience. It wasn't easy to recognize at the time.

My friend, the next time you find yourself facing a season of adversity, look for provision. Look for God's grace. Remember Jeremiah, who learned that even prison can be an umbrella of God's provision. Remember that He cares for you. He sees the bigger picture. Even when you cannot see how, remember that He is at work on your behalf.

With God, often bad news is really good news in disguise.

Notes

lesson 7

Jeremiah 38–44

Redefining Success

Mrs. Harding was nearly ninety years old when Evangeline and Archie McNeil first met her. As a retired Christian and Missionary Alliance missionary, she might have spent her time reading, resting, and enjoying what remained of her life. Instead, as World War II drew to a close, this elderly woman moved home to Portland, Oregon. Undaunted by age and nearly complete blindness, she began to seek God for her next assignment.

Mrs. Harding believed that the pastors of her day were a mentally lazy bunch, far too prone to preach opinion instead of fact. Too willing to rest instead of research. Too lazy to memorize the Scriptures. This situation needed correction, and she believed that God had called her to help these men grow in Christ.

And so this elderly widow opened her home to Portland area pastors and their wives and began to teach the Bible. Each week, she insisted that her students memorize Scripture, assigning long, sometimes book-length passages for public recitation.

For what she termed, "mental exercise," she interrupted her weekly teaching with long, multi-step math problems, demanding that the men calculate the answers in their heads and respond instantaneously. Mrs. Harding, demonstrating her own mental quickness, frequently answered these questions more rapidly than any of her younger students.

As a retired missionary, Mrs. Harding might have spent her time reading, resting, and enjoying what remained of her life. Instead, as World War II drew to a close, this elderly woman moved home to Portland, Oregon. . . . and began to seek God for her next assignment.

"You must exercise the mind," she insisted. "Or you will lose what little capacity you have." Mrs. Harding lived out her convictions, more than fifty years before such understanding became common medical truth.

Mrs. Harding was a woman of influence, unwilling to let her age, marital status, or physical handicap keep her from serving God.

Eventually Archie and Evangeline left Portland to open Cannon Beach Christian Conference Center. In the forty years after her husband died, Evangeline McNeil never forgot Mrs. Harding. In the old woman's home, Evangeline developed a love for scripture memory that forever equipped her for future service. Evangeline directed the conference center alone for nearly forty years.

Mrs. Harding was a woman of influence, using her unique gifts to shape others for Christ. This week, we'll discover what it means to be a person of influence.

Jeremiah influenced the world around him. Can we?

Jeremiah 38–44

DAY ONE

NEVER GIVE UP

Have you ever noticed that the pages of Scripture rarely reflect our contemporary values? Think about the emphasis American society places on power, prestige, accomplishment, and fiscal success. Interestingly, none of these values are reflected in Jeremiah's life. In fact, if I were to choose one word that most closely captures Jeremiah's ministry, I would use the word, "influence."

Jeremiah was a man of influence.

Influential men and women have many common attributes. In general, they are people who understand and respond to the authority over them. Often courageous and known for taking risks, their commitment to their work is complete; they hold nothing back. They are creative people who can envision completing a task—team players who often place greater emphasis on developing the gifts of those who serve with them than they do on exerting power over others.

In general, they are deeply compassionate people who care more about accomplishing a goal than they care about getting credit for reaching the goal. Influential men and women are faithful to their positions, willing to endure hardship and sacrifice. They deeply invest themselves—their time, their emotions, and their personal resources—in order to finish the tasks they have accepted.

Jeremiah, like many biblical heroes, was this kind of man. But as we come to lesson 7, we realize that his story is not yet over. He has more to accomplish, more difficulties to endure. Sometimes, even when we think we've made it through the worst, things continue to deteriorate.

Such is the case with Jeremiah. When we last left him, King Zedekiah had imprisoned our hero. Though Zedekiah no longer held Jeremiah in the dungeon, Jeremiah had been confined in the quarters of the palace guard. This week, our study opens with a complaint against Jeremiah.

> ***"... but I will rescue you from those you fear so much. Because you trusted me, I will give you your life as a reward. I will rescue you and keep you safe. I, the Lord, have spoken!"***
>
> ***Jeremiah 39:17***

📖 Begin by reading Jeremiah 38. As chapter 38 opens, what message was Jeremiah giving the people?

What charges did Shephatiah, Gedaliah (son of Pashhur), Jehucal, and Pashhur bring against Jeremiah? What did they say his message would do to the fighting men and the people?

____

____

____

____

What was the king's response? Does the king's response tell you something about his state of mind at this point?

____

____

____

You've probably felt like Zedekiah at some point in your life. Facing grief, or a frightening diagnosis, or a sudden, severe financial setback, you might have found yourself becoming passive, giving in to the ideas and suggestions of those around you. Whether the king felt hopeless, or suffered from depression we'll never know. Somehow he has come to the place of passivity, where he is no longer making his own decisions.

At this point Scripture tells us Jeremiah is *"taken from his cell"* (Jeremiah 38:6). If Jeremiah was actually living in his prison cell, why would the officials have felt the need to further silence him?

____

____

____

This is a great question to ponder. Obviously, something has happened that the writer of Jeremiah (most likely dictated by Jeremiah himself) has chosen to keep from us. Is Jeremiah sending messages to the people via his visitors? Is he yelling through the windows? Or, has his imprisonment stirred the public sentiment so much that the guards felt the need to hide him?

____

____

____

While we can't answer the question definitively, we can guess from the story that Jeremiah continued to influence people even while he was imprisoned. As you consider what made Jeremiah a problem to these men, think about yourself in the same situation.

How would you feel if your ministry made you a candidate for imprisonment? Would your emotions rule over your responses? I think I would struggle with feeling forgotten, perhaps a little betrayed by God. I might mutter, "I was serving you faithfully, Lord. What am I doing here?" I doubt I would continue to serve.

"So the officials took Jeremiah from his cell and lowered him by ropes into an empty cistern in the prison yard. It belonged to Malkijah, a member of the royal family. There was no water in the cistern, but there was a thick layer of mud at the bottom and Jeremiah sank down into it."

Jeremiah 38:6

____

____

____

But the evidence suggests that Jeremiah simply continued to do what he had always done. He continued to faithfully share the message God had given him.

Where did the officials put Jeremiah (38:6)? Describe the environment where Jeremiah found himself.

____

____

____

At this point, almost miraculously, something happens. Make some notes about who takes action. What does this person do?

____

____

____

As Ebed-melech speaks to the king, he mentions a situation in the city that would surely kill Jeremiah. What is it?

____

____

____

What does Ebed-melech do to help Jeremiah? Pay attention to the details about how this palace official, this Ethiopian, carries out his mission. What do Ebed-melech's actions tell you about this man?

____

____

____

JEREMIAH 38:12–13

Ebed-melech called down to Jeremiah, "Put these rags under your armpits to protect you from the ropes." Then when Jeremiah was ready, they pulled him out. So Jeremiah was returned to the courtyard of the guard—the palace prison—where he remained.

I can hardly express how much it tickles me that this Ethiopian intervenes on Jeremiah's behalf. Surely God used him; I'm quite certain that Jeremiah knew it too. Imagine standing partially submerged in a thick layer of mud, your eyes completely blinded by the sudden and complete darkness at the bottom of the well. While the men above you laugh, you hear the quiet but unmistakable scratching of a nearby rodent. And just as you are about to scream, you recognize a new sound, the sound of receding footsteps. The men who dropped you into this tomb have left you alone in the dark.

Perhaps then, like Joseph, Jeremiah called out, to his captors. "Don't leave me. I'll die down here. . . ."

But they left him, just the same.

How long did he stay in the well? An hour? A day? Three days? We don't know. Jeremiah stayed there at least until Ebed-melech heard about the situation and took action. Certainly Jeremiah must have struggled with his emotions down in the bottom of that hole. Did he worry about dying? Did he fear being alone? Was he relieved that his ministry was at last finished? Can you imagine his surprise when he heard the sound of ropes bouncing against the cistern's stone walls? Confused, he must have looked up and strained to identify the face backlighted by brilliant Middle Eastern sunlight.

Jeremiah must have felt confusion when he first heard the voice of Ebed-melech calling down the shaft. *"Put these rags under your armpits to protect you from the ropes."*

No doubt, Jeremiah realized that God had provided a way out of the cistern.

Think about this story from Ebed-melech's point of view. He must have understood that Jeremiah was a man of God. But Ebed-Melech was an outsider—not even a Jew! As an Ethiopian, not only is he a religious outsider, but it is likely that he was of a different race. Why would this black-skinned stranger stick his neck out for old Jeremiah? Things were dangerous in those days: people went to prison for speaking against the king. This palace official took a huge risk to go to the king and ask for mercy. After all, that kind of request certainly put Ebed-melech on Jeremiah's side.

Jeremiah had already been accused of treason.

Ebed-melech likely knew that the king had recently killed God's prophets. But what he didn't know or couldn't possibly understand was how his kindness would change the course of history. Because he cared for Jeremiah, all the rest of Jeremiah's ministry was recorded for us. Because Jeremiah survived his stay in the well, we enjoy Jeremiah's messages (including those which followed the destruction of the city), his accounts of the fall of Jerusalem, the book of Lamentations, and all of his prophecy concerning Babylon and Judah's neighboring nations.

Because of Ebed-melech, we get to watch God's faithful care for Jeremiah and Baruch. Because of Ebed-melech's courage—one man against the world—we see the world is changed.

Could you be that kind of person? That one faithful soul who does the right thing at the right time? The one who changes the course of history? Could you?

ANOTHER HERO

"Let's go across to the outpost of those pagans," Jonathan said to his armor bearer. "Perhaps the Lord will help us, for nothing can hinder the Lord. He can win a battle whether he has many warriors or only a few!"

"Do what you think is best," the armor bearer replied. "I'm with you completely, whatever you decide." (1 Samuel 14:6–7)

INFLUENCING THE KING

Jeremiah 38–44

DAY TWO

In the second half of chapter 38, we witness a clandestine meeting between Jeremiah and a very important citizen. Who meets with Jeremiah (38:14)?

Remember this is the king who has allowed Jeremiah to be imprisoned and dropped into a cistern. Just as the king is about to make his request, Jeremiah responds. Note his response.

Thinking about these words in light of Jeremiah's early days of ministry, do Jeremiah's words indicate a change in his outlook? Do you think he is becoming more brave? More careless? Hopeless for others or for his own influence?

King Zedekiah never gets to ask his question. Before he is able to speak, Jeremiah gives him an ultimatum. What is it?

What seems to be Zedekiah's secret fear (38:19)?

Because the chapters in the book of Jeremiah appear out of order, we have difficulty getting a clear picture of King Zedekiah. Jeremiah records a series of exchanges between this king and himself. In chapter 34, Jeremiah assures the king that he will not die in war, but peacefully, in exile. As we read chapter 38 with the understanding that this chapter could also be out of sequence, we can't be absolutely certain that Zedekiah has yet heard this message about his own fate. Perhaps this is why he is afraid of being killed by the Judeans in exile. Or, perhaps he has heard the message, but his fear is louder than his faith. Fear does have a way of shouting at us.

Jeremiah's answer to the king is simple, *"Obey the Lord."* Over and over, Jeremiah has told the king that the Babylonians will take the city. Over and over, Jeremiah appeals to Zedekiah, *Accept your fate. . . . Obey the* L*ORD. . . . Surrender to the Babylonians.*

From this account in chapter 38, we have no idea what Zedekiah will choose. Only later, as the city falls, does the king reveal his own foolishness. Before he leaves Jeremiah, Zedekiah asks another question. What is it? How does Jeremiah respond? (See 38:24–27.)

In Isaiah 8:12, the prophet says, *"Do not be afraid that some plan conceived behind closed doors will be the end of you. Do not fear anything except the* L*ORD Almighty. He alone is the Holy One. If you fear him, you need fear nothing else."* As you work on this Bible study, what is it that you fear most? Do those who love you know what you are afraid of? What steps could you take to replace

Did You Know?

SIEGE WARFARE

By the time of Nebuchadnezzar, the Babylonians had already perfected siege warfare. Most cities in Mesopotamia were surrounded by tall, thick walls, built on wide bases—some as much as thirty-four meters thick.

The weakest points of every walled city are the gates. The Assyrians, who preceded the Babylonians, introduced the three-fold technique of siege. The entire operation depended on organization of the troops; each division of soldiers carefully trained to act under the protection of others as they did their part to break through the city walls.

your secret fear with a healthy fear of God?

Zedekiah clearly doesn't want his palace officials to know that he has met with Jeremiah. Why do you think Zedekiah was so desperate to keep his meeting a secret?

What kinds of things might Zedekiah have said to his palace officials about Jeremiah? What does this secret meeting imply that he really thinks?

I like to keep this story in mind when I face opposition. Over years of ministry, I've discovered, as Jeremiah did, that a person's outward response is not always indicative of his inward state. Often, even as people loudly object to your biblical perspective, inside they consider your words. When you add time and patience to the work of the Holy Spirit, and the Word of God, things happen! Kings repent. Believers change their ways. Divisive spirits vanish. Healing begins.

Over the years of his ministry, King Zedekiah had listened to Jeremiah. Some part of the king believed that Jeremiah spoke for God. Though he might not admit it outwardly, the king had been influenced.

Don't let your audience's outward resistance discourage you from continued godly input. You never know what influence your words may have!

Later, the palace officials question Jeremiah, who keeps the king's big secret. Why do you think that Jeremiah cooperated with the king? What might have happened otherwise?

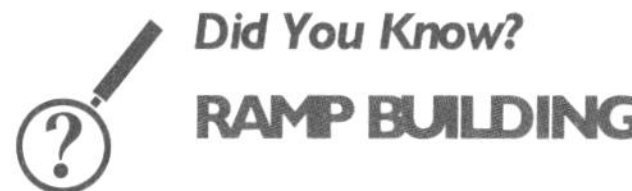

Did You Know?

RAMP BUILDING

In Babylonian warfare, engineers designed ramps, using sophisticated mathematical calculations to determine the exact volume of earth needed for ramps reaching the tops of city walls. Using these advanced techniques, they determined both the number of soldiers needed to move the earth and the number of work days required. One historical document calculates five twelve-hour days for 9,500 men to build a ramp to the top of a 22-meter wall.

Did You Know?

BATTERING RAM

In his essay titled "History of Mesopotamian Siege Science," Apiladey ApilSin explains that siege warfare was well established early in the Assyrian empire. Since most major cities were walled, siege warfare centered on breaching the walls using the following techniques:

Soldiers sometimes used a battering ram so heavy that it needed six wheels for support. It was covered with wet animal skins to keep it from burning, and was about 15 feet long. The front held a turret, hiding archers whose sole job was to defend the ram during battle. These heavy battering rams were used on the city gates, while similar but lighter rams were moved up the siege ramp to batter through thinner upper city walls.

(http://www.ancientworlds.net/aw/Post/238455)

Jeremiah 38–44

DAY THREE

THE CITY FALLS

We're nearly finished with our study of Jeremiah. We've watched God choose this young man to serve him. We've seen Jeremiah struggle with the people's response. We've witnessed God's correction of Jeremiah. And we've observed some of the word pictures God

Did You Know?

SAPPING

According to Apiladey ApilSin, ancient warfare strategy involved **sapping.** Under the protection of armor and shields, soldiers tunneled into the wall surrounding a city. As they dug, they built temporary supports, which held up the wall above them. Then, just before they reached the inside surface, they set fire to the supports, which caused the entire wall above the tunnel to collapse. Thus soldiers entered the city over the fallen wall.

Normally, royalty (like King Nebuchadnezzar) did not lead these assault teams, but instead led a team of chariots, driven by other aristocrats. Together, the aristocrats chased down and eliminated any persons escaping from the besieged city.

(http://www.ancientworlds.net/aw/Post/238455)

gives Jeremiah to illustrate his messages. Now, the story is about to come to a dramatic close. Everything that Jeremiah has predicted is about to come true. Yet, in spite of the downward spiral in Jerusalem, God is not finished with Jeremiah. Let's look closely at what follows.

📖 Using Jeremiah 39:1–3, note how long it took for Nebuchadnezzar to conquer Jerusalem. Check your work by comparing these numbers with the same calculations from Jeremiah 52:4–6.

____

Being the courageous king that he was, after months of siege, Zedekiah shows his true colors. What does Zedekiah do when he sees the Babylonians march into town?

____

____

____

What happened to Zedekiah? Compare what happened to the king to Jeremiah's prediction. Was Jeremiah's prediction correct? Why or why not?

____

____

____

Remember that Zedekiah's secret fear centered around being abused by the captives in Babylon. Jeremiah's promise of safety was conditional on the king's surrender to the Babylonian army. In fact, Jeremiah says, "*If you surrender, you and your family will live,*" and it will "*go well with you.*" But Zedekiah chooses not to surrender. He has his army fight until the city is defeated, and then he tries to escape. The Babylonians chase the king and capture him outside the city. His punishment is to watch his sons and all the nobles of Jerusalem die. Then he is blinded and taken as captive to Babylon.

What a horrible experience for Zedekiah! Yet, we cannot mistake God's grace in his life. God gave this king an opportunity to save himself and his family. Through Jeremiah God warns Zedekiah and then gives him two and a half years to consider the opportunity for surrender.

📖 In Jeremiah 39:8, we read what happened to Jerusalem. What happened to the city? Remember that the army of Judah had taken apart the city buildings to reinforce the city's wall. However, their work did not protect them from the Babylonians. What did Nebuzaradan do?

____

____

____

Imagine how it might feel to watch your city burn to the ground. Think of the pain of seeing the homes belonging to friends and neighbors burn. Imagine finding people you love lying in the street, killed by famine or war. Would you have felt despair? Might you have lost your faith? Would you be angry with your people because of their disobedience? Angry with God because of His extreme cruelty? Imagine how Jeremiah felt, knowing that it all might have been avoided.

What happened to the people living in Jerusalem? What happened to the poorest of the people in Judah (39:10)?

Where was Jeremiah at the time the city fell (39:14)?

What did the conquering army do with Jeremiah (39:14)?

Once again, we can allow ourselves some speculation here, as the text doesn't afford any juicy details. Did you notice that Nebuchadnezzar sends his army officers looking for Jeremiah by name? How do you think Nebuchadnezzar knew about Jeremiah?

Don't forget; according to 2 Kings, there have already been several deportations of citizens from Jerusalem to Babylon, The first happened under Jehoiakim's reign. The second occurred during Jehoiakin's reign. The last deportation occurred after Jerusalem was finally destroyed. It is possible that some of these newly transported citizens talked about Jeremiah. Or perhaps Zedekiah, who has made the trip to Babylon at least once, might have complained about Jeremiah in some official conversation. We know that Daniel, who was an advisor to Nebuchadnezzar, knew about Jeremiah. Daniel 9:2 records Daniel's reading the words of Jeremiah, the Prophet. Perhaps Daniel is the source of the Babylonian king's information.

Somehow, Nebuchadnezzar had already heard about Jeremiah and determined that the prophet was no threat to the Babylonians. Whatever the source, whatever the reason, I'm certain that God used Nebuchadnezzar to protect his beloved and faithful prophet when everything around him went up in smoke.

Did You Know?

PASSIVE SIEGE

When the expense or difficulty of an active siege became prohibitive, ancient armies sometimes chose to install a passive siege. By surrounding a city, and building a second wall surrounding the first (thus eliminating gates and escape routes for the besieged city) the enemy army ensured that the city had no source of food beyond what it had already stored.

In this case, famine usually caused the conflict to end, either by surrender or death. Passive siege was exorbitantly expensive, requiring the assaulting nation to feed a large army for many months—even years. Boredom became a problem as well. The besieging army had little to do, and sometimes struggled to remain vigilant against escaping citizens or royalty. This kind of boredom may even have kept attacking armies from anticipating and defending themselves against sorties from the city. (http://www.ancientworlds.net/aw/Post/238455) For more information about ancient warfare, see "Ancient Siege Warfare" by Paul Bently Kern.

After Jerusalem Fell

Jeremiah 38–44

DAY FOUR

We're going to wrap this week up by discovering what Paul Harvey would call, "the rest of the story." Many of the characters in this book have intrigued and challenged us. As the city falls into Nebuchadnezzar's hands, we might worry about these heroes, these men who have helped Jeremiah; but God is faithful. And God is kind to us in that He lets us know what happened to them after the city fell. As I watch His care for these men, I find myself very encouraged. God does not forget those who serve Him. He will never forget me! Let's find out what happened.

Did You Know?

THE MARCH TO BABYLON

According to the *Jewish Encyclopedia*, Nebuchadnezzar was merciless toward conquered peoples. He ordered that Judean exiles marching to Babylon would not be allowed to stop, even for a moment. The king feared that if they were allowed to rest, they would repent and call upon their God, who would then come to rescue them.

This demonstrates remarkable insight for a man not raised in the Jewish culture.

In order to increase the misery of his captives, Nebuchadnezzar had rolls of the Torah torn and made into sacks, which he filled with sand and made the captives carry all the way to their new home.

Nebuchadnezzar did not feel safe until the exiles reached the Euphrates River—the boundary line of Babylon. According to historical documents, when the captives arrived, he left the princes of Judah chained and naked by the river, while he enjoyed a great feast on board his ship.

(http://www.jewishencyclopedia.com/view.jsp?artid=154&letter=N)

Remember Ebed-melech? He was the kind Ethiopian who fetched Jeremiah from the bottom of the cistern. God remembers his kindness and gives Jeremiah a message just for the Ethiopian (39:15–18). In the space below, paraphrase the message. What emotions did Ebed-melech feel? How do you think it felt to this man to have his most private emotions addressed by Jeremiah in this message from God? This passage reminds us that God knows our secret thoughts and fears. You need not hide your concerns from Him; He already knows.

____

____

____

____

____

📖 Where did Nebuzaradan, captain of the Babylonian guard find Jeremiah (40:1)? What does this Babylonian say caused the disaster in the city? What do his words tell you about the rumors that must have been floating around before the city fell?

____

____

____

____

📖 What choices does Nebuzaradan offer Jeremiah (40:4–5)?

____

____

Who had been named Governor of Judah?

____

I love it when a careful reading of the text clarifies perplexing issues. In chapter 38, Gedaliah is one of the men who bring charges against Jeremiah. However, we know from the text that the Gedaliah, who becomes governor of Judah (40:6) is not this same man. How do we know?

____

____

What gifts does Nebuzaradan give Jeremiah (40:5)?

____

At first glance, Jeremiah 39 and 40 seem to tell differing stories of what happened to Jeremiah. But perhaps I can help you see these accounts in a new light. Remember in Genesis 1, the author tells us that on the sixth day God created man. But in chapter 2, the author relates this story again, only the second time he gives us more detail. These two stories are not different stories, but the same story told twice—each from a different perspective.

I believe that this same thing happens in the Jeremiah account. In chapter 39 we read the Reader's Digest abridged version. Nebuchadnezzar tells Nebuzaradan to look for Jeremiah. The king's officials send messages to get Jeremiah out of prison and put him in the care of Gedaliah, the newly-appointed governor of Judah.

But in chapter 40, the account is told again with color and detail, even going so far as to give us an account of Nebuzaradan's conversation with Jeremiah when at last he is found. I would guess that Nebuchadnezzar's officers could not find Jeremiah in prison. Perhaps, without being recognized by the officer in charge, Jeremiah had already been shuffled off to the staging area where the captives were readied to travel. Eventually, after Nebuchadnezzar's men searched for him, Jeremiah was found in Ramah. You might be interested to know that there were five towns in Judah with the name "Ramah" at the time of the fall of Jerusalem. However, history tells us that Nebuchadnezzar used the town of **Ramah of Benjamin** (located just five miles north of Jerusalem) as the place from which he sent all his Judean captives to Babylon.

Remember that Nebuzaradan represents a bitter enemy of Judah. He is part of the army that has destroyed the city and desecrated the Temple. Due to siege and war, Nebuzaradan has caused the death of huge numbers of Jews living in Jerusalem. Isn't it interesting that in Jeremiah's case, God uses this evil man from a pagan nation to directly provide for Jeremiah? In fact, through Nebuzaradan, God blesses Jeremiah with the promise of protection, the freedom to choose where he would live, and with provisions of food and money. All these things are given to Jeremiah via the kindness of this enemy.

APPLY Have you experienced times when God used an enemy—of the Church, of ministry, of God—to bless you? When?

____

____

____

____

____

____

Where did Jeremiah choose to go (40:6)?

____

Do you remember Baruch, the man to whom Jeremiah dictated the scroll of God's messages? Not only did Baruch write all the messages down, but he also went to the Temple and read the messages aloud. And then, after the king destroyed the scroll, Baruch wrote it all down a second time.

Baruch suffered arrest with Jeremiah and perhaps, by siding with him, sacrificed his future as an official in the king's court. In hindsight, we know that the king's court would not last very long. But Baruch certainly had no such assurance. From his point of view, siding with Jeremiah might have cost him his life.

Look at Jeremiah chapter 45, where the entire chapter is a short message to our faithful Baruch. What does God say that might reveal Baruch's inner desire? What promise does He make to Baruch?

____

____

____

DESTRUCTION OF THE CITY

Likewise, all the leaders of the priests and the people became more and more unfaithful. They followed all the pagan practices of the surrounding nations, desecrating the Temple of the Lord that had been consecrated in Jerusalem.

The Lord, the God of their ancestors, repeatedly sent his prophets to warn them, for he had compassion on his people and his Temple. But the people mocked these messengers of God and despised their words. They scoffed at the prophets until the Lord's anger could no longer be restrained and nothing could be done.

So the Lord brought the king of Babylon against them. The Babylonians killed Judah's young men, even chasing after them into the Temple. They had no pity on the people, killing both young men and young women, the old and the infirm. God handed all of them over to Nebuchadnezzar. . . . Then his army burned the Temple of God, tore down the walls of Jerusalem, burned all the palaces, and completely destroyed everything of value. (2 Chronicles 36:14–17, 19)

THE CITY LAYS DESOLATE

The few who survived were taken as exiles to Babylon, and they became servants to the king and his sons until the kingdom of Persia came to power.

So the message of the Lord spoken through Jeremiah was fulfilled. The land finally enjoyed its Sabbath rest, lying desolate until the seventy years were fulfilled, just as the prophet had said. (2 Chronicles 36:19–21)

From God's message to Baruch, do you detect a warning for your own life? What is it?

____

____

Jeremiah 38–44

DAY FIVE

JEREMIAH IS KIDNAPPED

Now we must take a small side trip. In order to understand the rest of the book of Jeremiah, we must understand the political intrigue surrounding the fall of Jerusalem. Rather than make you dig these details out of the text by yourself, I'll summarize the story for you.

From your study, you know that after Jerusalem is destroyed, most of the population of Judah is deported to Babylon, a miserable walk of more than five hundred miles (as the crow flies). Only a few of the poorest people have been left in the land. The city, burned, destroyed, and uninhabitable, is nearly empty.

At the beginning of chapter 40, the Babylonians allow Jeremiah to choose where he wants to go. Jeremiah moves to Mitzpah with Gedaliah, the man Nebuchadnezzar had appointed governor of Judah. This governorship is a puppet position.

Gedaliah encourages all the people who have survived to come out of hiding and surrender to the Babylonians. To do so, he tells them, is to live in peace in the land. He tells them to harvest the crops, serve the king, and promises that all will go well with them.

Some of these surviving Judeans warn Gedaliah of an insurgent plot against his life. Gedaliah ignores their warning and is murdered by insurrectionists; the murderers capture the people left in Judah and take off with them. A small sortie goes after the Governor's murderers and recovers the lost captives.

This remnant of rescuers and captives is now terrified of Babylonian reprisal. After all, someone has slain Nebuchadnezzar's appointed official. In fear, they decide to flee to Egypt, where they believe they will be safe from Nebuchadnezzar.

But before they leave, they visit Jeremiah.

In Jeremiah 42:1, this group of rescuers and captives comes to Jeremiah and asks for something. What is it? What exactly do they want to know?

____

____

____

What do they promise Jeremiah? Notice that this promise is not extracted or demanded by Jeremiah. It is a promise freely given. Why do you think they make this promise?

REBELLION CONTINUES

So Johanan and the other guerrilla leaders and all the people refused to obey the Lord's command to stay in Judah. Johanan and the other leaders took with them all the people who had returned from the nearby countries to which they had fled. In the crowd were men, women, and children, the king's daughters, and all those whom Nebuzaradan, the captain of the guard, had left with Gedaliah. The prophet Jeremiah and Baruch were also included. The people refused to obey the voice of the Lord and went to Egypt, going as far as the city of Tahpanhes. (Jeremiah 43:4–7)

📖 As requested, Jeremiah intercedes on their behalf. How long does Jeremiah wait for the Lord's answer (42:7)? When you pray, how long are you willing to wait for an answer? Does it surprise you to see this biblical hero waiting, just like you, for God's answer?

When God responds to Jeremiah, He gives one simple command. What is it?

Then, because He is gracious, God amplifies His answer, associating the command with a promise. He gives the people a series of consequences. In the space below, list the consequences of both obedience and disobedience. Why do you think God added these consequences to His answer? Do you think that these people had enough information to make a wise decision?

Consequences of Obedience:

Consequences of Disobedience:

📖 In Jeremiah 42:21, Jeremiah predicts what the people will do. What does he predict? What does he say about their character?

What do the people choose? Who is with them? Where do they go (43:4–8)?

As tempting as it is to criticize this Judean remnant, I recognize myself in them. How often do I seek God's direction, making vain promises to obey, no matter what the cost? And then, do I obey? Or do I let my own fear cloud my judgment? It's so easy, isn't it, to let our imagination and fear get the better of us? In our mind's eye, we can clearly picture every unpleasant consequence of obeying God. We imagine being rejected, ridiculed, or laughed at. We picture losing our jobs, fracturing our family or offending someone we love.

If only we were as good at picturing the positive outcome of obedience. If we were the remnant, we might picture gathering our own crops, caring for healthy animals, watching the rain come in due season. We could picture feasts and weddings and celebrations.

Instead, these people could picture only Babylonian retaliation. With that picture in mind, they make one last fatal choice.

For most of us, moving to Egypt with this rebellious, unbelieving remnant would be the last straw. After forty years of faithful and sacrificial ministry, Jeremiah deserves a break doesn't he? He had continually given the people God's messages. He's lived a restricted life, entirely focused on God and his work. When Jeremiah finds himself living with the Judeans in northern Egypt, I think he'd have every right to give up. After all, the worst has come. The king of Judah has ignored him. The city is destroyed. The people are gone. And now this! Jeremiah finds himself taken against his will to Egypt.

SIX HUNDRED YEARS LATER . . .

"You stubborn people! You are heathen at heart and deaf to the truth. Must you forever resist the Holy Spirit? That's what your ancestors did, and so do you! Name one prophet your ancestors didn't persecute! They even killed the ones who predicted the coming of the Righteous One—the Messiah whom you betrayed and murdered. You deliberately disobeyed God's law, even though you received it from the hands of angels." (Stephen, the first martyr, in Acts 7:51–53)

Who wouldn't want to quit?

But Jeremiah does not give up. Instead, he continues to deliver God's messages and plead with the people to turn from their stubborn determination to do evil. In chapter 44, Jeremiah recites God's complaints against Jerusalem and reviews what has happened to her people. To these complaints, Jeremiah adds God's complaints against the people who have fled to Egypt.

📖 In Jeremiah 44:8, Jeremiah lists a specific charge against the people. What is it?

Have the people learned anything from the destruction of Jerusalem?

📖 How do the people answer Jeremiah's charges (44:16–19)?

Their response reminds me of rebellious children. "I won't do it," they say, stamping their feet. "You can't make me!" How foolish these people are. Having lived through God's correction of Judah, how can they doubt His response to their continued idolatry? Though it seems impossible that we would ever find ourselves in these same disobedient and rebellious shoes, we must pay attention to these foolish people. Only by making every effort to combine godly obedience with prayer and humility, can we keep ourselves safe. Without these elements, we might find ourselves languishing in the Egypt of disobedience.

📖 What does God promise will happen to the remnant living in Egypt (44:11–12, 27–28)?

____

____

As I Follow God:
At the end of every summer, the potted plants on my deck begin to look a little wilted. I get bored with caring for my flowers. A vacation or two diverts my attention. More than once a book deadline has sapped my energy. Here and there, I forget to water. As late summer turns to fall, faded flowers cling to crisp leaves. Dehydration drives some of my annuals to seed.

When that happens, I know I must do something drastic to bring life back into my garden. I must remove the dead blossoms, pick off the dried leaves, add water, and fertilize thoroughly. But every year, as I'm carefully removing the faded flowers, I get tired. Part of me wants to take my garden shears and give all my plants a drastic haircut.

Just cut it all back, I think.

Take out the good with the bad. Force the plants to start over. After all, selective trimming takes time and care. I don't have that kind of patience. I just want to finish and move on. I would; but late in the season, summer annuals don't have time to rebound from that kind of drastic treatment. If I gave in to my urges, I wouldn't have a single bloom before winter.

Fortunately for us all, God takes greater care with his people than I take with my garden.

Even in the midst of Judah's drastic correction, God did not sweep everyone away. He did not trim the whole plant. He selected the individuals who would travel to Babylon. He selected the ones who would stay. We know this from Jeremiah's carefully stated messages to Baruch and to Ebed-melech. These men, who had taken great risks to serve God, did not experience the severe punishment that was meted out to the rest of the people. Jeremiah, God's faithful servant, not only survived the long siege and initial destruction of the city, but also the political unrest that followed. When rebellious insurgents murdered governor Gedaliah, Jeremiah (who was staying with him) remained safe.

Why is this important to me?

Because I take great comfort in knowing that situations don't get out of hand with God. God, for the sake of His time, or energy, or interest, never gives massive, uncontrolled correction. After studying this section of Jeremiah, I can

THE EXILE BEGINS

Zedekiah was twenty-one years old when he became king, and he reigned in Jerusalem eleven years. His mother was Hamutal, the daughter of Jeremiah from Libnah. But Zedekiah did what was evil in the Lord's sight, just as Jehoiakim had done. These things happened because of the Lord's anger against the people of Jerusalem and Judah, until he finally banished them from his presence and sent them into exile. Zedekiah rebelled against the king of Babylon. (2 Kings 24:18–20)

be certain that I will never become unintentionally caught up in some correction that was meant for "others" and not for me.

Of course Jeremiah, Baruch and Ebed-Melech all lived in a time of severe difficulty. They lived through siege, famine, and drought. They were not entirely removed from the culture and circumstances around them. Each of them would probably testify that times were very difficult. They might admit that they struggled with worry and fear. Undoubtedly, they wondered how it would all come out.

But they would also give glory to God—because God never allowed the circumstances to destroy them. At every moment, even when things seemed completely random and out of control, God had not forgotten them!

He will not forget us either!

Notes

Notes

Jeremiah 45–52

God Keeps His Word

Shortly after a disaster took her father's life at sea, Karen Jacobsen explained his philosophy to a local news reporter. Dad did what he'd always promised. His job was to take care of his crew.

Shortly after a disaster took her father's life at sea, Karen Jacobsen explained his philosophy to a local news reporter. Dad did what he'd always promised. His job was to take care of his crew.

Shortly before dawn on Easter Sunday, 2008, the men on board the *Alaska Ranger* realized their ship was going to sink. After losing control of the rudder, the 120-foot ship began taking on water and was soon foundering in twenty-foot seas. With no other options, captain Jacobsen immediately sent a mayday message and ordered his men to don survival suits and begin launching life rafts. Then, in the pre-dawn darkness, the *Alaska Ranger's* captain helped his crew abandon the sinking vessel and enter the water.

The *Ranger* sank in the Bering Sea, 120 miles west of Dutch Harbor, Alaska. Forty-two of the forty-seven crewmen were later plucked out of the water by a US Coast Guard helicopter with the assistance of a sister ship, *The Alaska Warrior*. The rescue, in heavy seas and twenty-five-knot winds, involved falling snow and sea temperatures of twenty-nine degrees Fahrenheit. It became one of the largest cold-water rescues in the Coast Guard's history, with at least thirteen individual survivors bobbing in high seas, stretched out along a one-mile line.

For the families of the survivors, the story has a happy ending. For Captain Eric Peter Jacobsen's family, the story ends quite differently. Jacobson died after ensuring that each of his crew made it safely into the water. According to a Seattle news report, shortly after the ship sank, Karen Jacobsen, the captain's daughter, discussed her father's promise to care for his men:

"I think that's the way he would have wanted to go, you know, saving other people, putting others before himself," Karen Jacobsen said. "I think he was a hero and someone doing his job. It was his job to be a hero if necessary."

Eric Jacobson promised to take care of his men. He kept his promise, even when it cost him his life.

For the past seven weeks, we've studied God's promises to His people, given through the prophet, Jeremiah. In this lesson we'll look at the ways God kept those promises. As we see God's faithfulness in the past, may we learn to trust His faithfulness in promises that He has yet to fulfill.

Enjoy this last look at the Book of Jeremiah!

Jeremiah 45–52

DAY ONE

GOD DUPLICATES HIS MESSAGE

"For the time is coming when I will restore the fortunes of my people of Israel and Judah. I will bring them home to this land that I gave to their ancestors, and they will possess it again. I, the Lord, have spoken!"

Jeremiah 30:3

Normally, a study of any Bible book ends with that book's final chapter. But in this case, ending there would leave students hanging, especially considering the depth and detail of Jeremiah's prophecy. Wouldn't you like to know what happened to Babylon? And what about the captives? Did they return as God promised? Did they rebuild Jerusalem? And what about the Temple?

Instead of leaving our study where the book ends, with Jeremiah in Egypt waiting for the Babylonians, let's move forward seventy years, and see if God's promises proved true. Were Jeremiah's words fulfilled by events still to come?

In order to answer these questions, we'll need to carefully examine other books of the Bible where different experiences and perspectives give clear accounts of the years following Jeremiah's abduction and transport to Egypt. We'll look at references to Jeremiah's words, at historical accounts, and also at New Testament passages. All in all, I think you'll be amazed to put the pieces of this complex puzzle together. And once you've finished, you'll find a new appreciation both for God and for his Word.

You remember from our study that the Babylonians overcame Judah three times. In the first invasion, Nebuchadnezzar conquered Judah (then under Jehoiakim's leadership) and exacted a financial tribute; at that time, he also took some of the Temple treasures back to Babylon. During all of Jehoiakim's reign, the Babylonians were in charge of the region. Bands of soldiers from the Babylonian, Aramean, Moabite and Ammonite armies kept Jerusalem under constant tension. Second Chronicles tells us that Jehoiakim eventually went to Babylon in chains, though it makes no mention of when exactly this occurred.

After his deportation, Jehoiakim's, son, Jehoiakin, became king. Three months into Jehoiakin's reign, Nebuchadnezzar returned to Judah and besieged the city of Jerusalem. After this second invasion, he deported King Jehoiakin and his nobles to Babylon. According to 2 Kings 24:14, Nebuchadnezzar took, *"ten thousand captives from Jerusalem, including all the princes and the best of the soldiers, craftsmen, and smiths. So only the poorest people were left in the land."*

Nebuchadnezzar then appointed Jehoiakin's uncle, Mattaniah, as a Babylonian vassal, changing his name to Zedekiah. Zedekiah reigned only nine years before he rebelled against Babylonian rule. At that point, Nebuchadnezzar returned for the third time and laid siege to Jerusalem. Two and a half years later, his men completely destroyed the city. Second Chronicles 36:20–21 describes this deportation in these words, *"The few who survivived were taken away to Babylon, and they became servants to the king and his sons until the kingdom of Persia came to power. So the message of the LORD spoken through Jeremiah was fulfilled. . . ."*

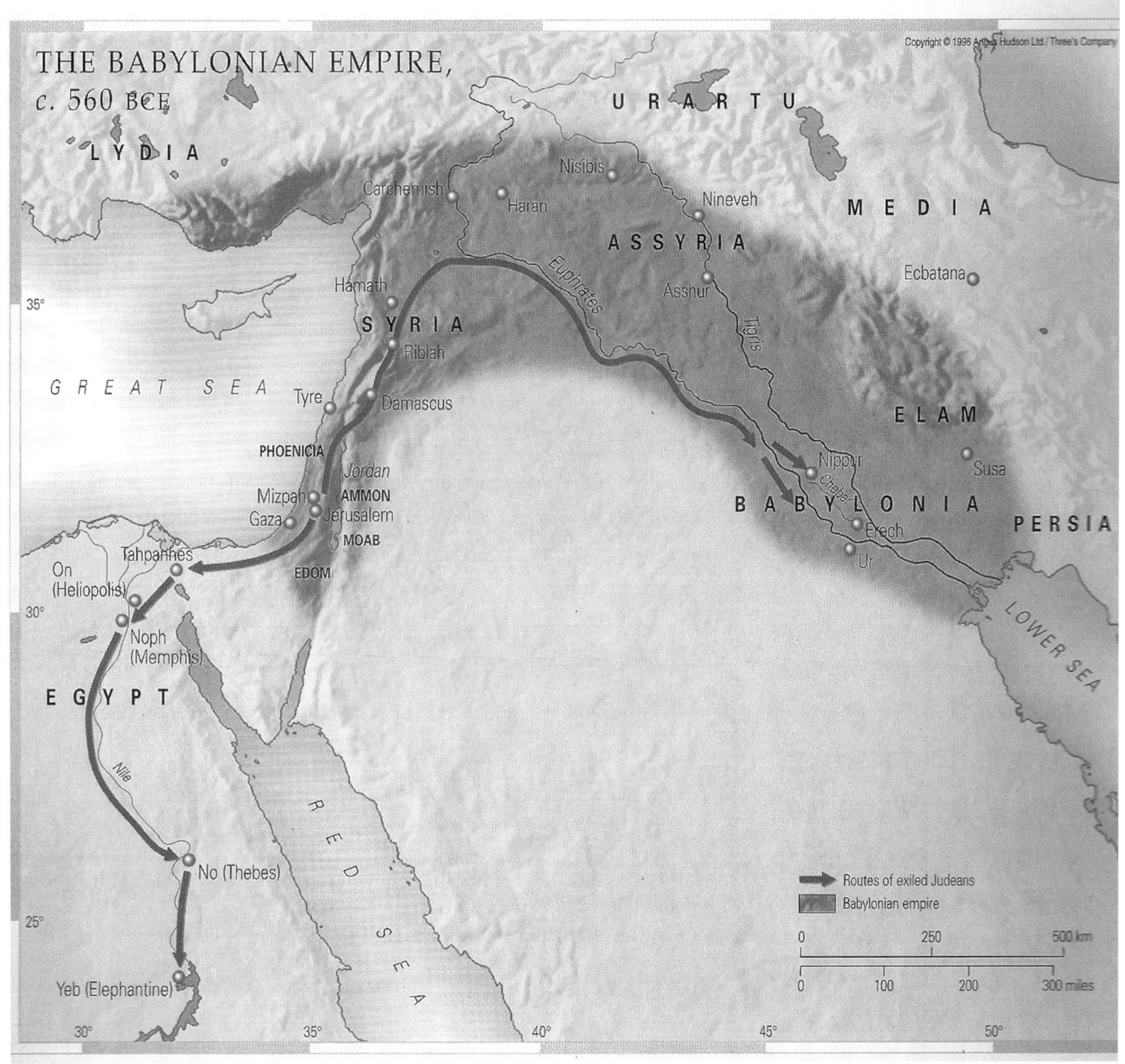

Be patient with this week's study. Answer your questions carefully, and you'll be amazed at what you discover!

📖 According to Ezekiel 1:1, where did Ezekiel minister? Ezekiel gives us a timeline in a kind of "back door" way. Using his date along with your chart of the **Last Kings of Judah** (p. 142), record which king was actually reigning in Jerusalem as the Book of Ezekiel opens.

📖 According to Ezekiel 1:1; 3:4, 10, to whom was Ezekiel supposed to speak?

____

📖 In Ezekiel 29:19–20, what event does Ezekiel prophecy? God says in this prophecy that He will reward Nebuchadnezzar for something. What is the reward? And what is it for?

____

____

____

I believe that God tells us much about His character by showing us His work through the prophet Ezekiel. Remember that ten thousand of God's people have already been taken into captivity. But God does not leave them in Babylon alone. Instead, he calls another prophet from among them, using Ezekiel to bring his people to repentance.

In Ezekiel 2:6–7, God tells his prophet, *"Son of man, do not fear them. Don't be afraid even though their threats are sharp as thorns and barbed like briers, and they sting like scorpions. . . . For remember, they are rebels! You must give them my messages whether they listen or not. But they won't listen, for they are completely rebellious!"*

How familiar are these words! Both Jeremiah and Ezekiel are working with the same audience—the stubborn and rebellious people of God.

Isn't it interesting that both Jeremiah (in Judah) and Ezekiel (more than five hundred miles away, in Babylon) both warn of the same destruction for Egypt? Why do you think God gave **both** of these men these words? Why do you think it was recorded twice?

____

____

____

"The Lord first gave messages to Jeremiah during the thirteenth year of the reign of Josiah son of Amon, king of Judah."

Jeremiah 1:2

📖 Now look at Ezekiel 39:25–29. What promise is given here?

____

____

____

In this passage God states that He will have mercy on Israel. What reason does He give for His action? Why do you think God gives Ezekiel, now in exile, this particular word for his fellow exiles?

____

____

____

Have you ever experienced the Lord's correction? By this, I don't mean simply living through a difficult season, but a direct correction—one where you knew that you were experiencing correction because of some specific act of disobedience. Perhaps then, you can imagine how desperately someone in that place needs hope. The hope that you might be restored. Hope for forgiveness. Hope that God had not forgotten you. This is the place where the men and women living in Babylon now found themselves.

Like us, they needed to know that God remembered them, that He had not forever rejected them for their disobedience. They needed hope! I believe that God sent Ezekiel to bring them hope.

God used these men, both Jeremiah and Ezekiel, to reach two different audiences. Jeremiah spoke to those still remaining in Judah, and Ezekiel to those already captive. Remember that eventually most of these people would end up together in Babylon. There it might have comforted them to know that these two prophets had both predicted the same captivity and eventual deliverance.

Daniel Experiences Captivity

Jeremiah 45–52

DAY TWO

Do you remember our discussion about point of view? While Jeremiah kept his account restricted to the things he saw and experienced, we can learn more about the Babylonian captivity from the records of the captives themselves. Today, we're going to look at the biblical account of one of the young men who was among the first group taken to Babylon. Let's begin by reading Daniel 1:1–5. When did Daniel go to Babylon? In general terms, how old was he when he was taken captive?

____

____

For what position did the Babylonians train him?

____

____

____

"The king said to Daniel, 'Truly, your God is the greatest of gods, the Lord over kings, a revealer of mysteries, for you have been able to reveal this secret.' "

Daniel 2:47

Using the first verse of the Book of Jeremiah, along with your chart depicting the Last Kings of Judah (p. 142), calculate the number of years that Jeremiah had been preaching before Daniel was deported to Babylon.

Interestingly, the books of Kings and Chronicles do not mention that Nebuchadnezzar took captives other than Judah's king when he first demanded tribute from Judah. In 2 Kings 24, the author tells us that when Jehoiakim (the first king to encounter Nebuchadnezzar) died, his son became king in his place. However, 2 Chronicles 36:6 tells us that Jehoiakim was taken to Babylon in chains. Perhaps Jehoiakim died in Babylon, and his son in Judah was then crowned king.

As for other captives, only Daniel provides that information. Adding his account to those of Kings and Chronicles, we know that Babylon took three waves of captives away from Israel during its season of dominion over Judah.

While we aren't exactly sure what Nebuchadnezzar had in mind for the young men taken with Daniel, we can guess from their qualifications and training—in literature, language, and knowledge—that Nebuchadnezzar intended to use these young captives as advisors to the royal court.

DANIEL IS CHOSEN

During the third year of King Jehoiakim's reign in Judah, King Nebuchadnezzar of Babylon came to Jerusalem and besieged it. The Lord gave him victory over King Jehoiakim of Judah and permitted him to take some of the sacred objects from the Temple of God.... Then the king ordered Ashpenaz, his chief of staff, to bring to the palace some of the young men of Judah's royal family and other noble families, who had been brought to Babylon as captives. "Select only strong, healthy, and good-looking young men," he said. "Make sure they are well versed in every branch of learning, are gifted with knowledge and good judgment, and are suited to serve in the royal palace. Train these young men in the language and literature of Babylon. (Daniel 1:1–4)

📖 Look at Daniel 1:18–20. Who interviewed the young men? What were his conclusions about Daniel and his friends?

____

____

____

Isn't it interesting that at the same time Jeremiah is begging the people in Jerusalem to repent, our friend Daniel has found a position as advisor to King Nebuchadnezzar? Over the course of his life, Daniel experiences a long series of difficulties in his relationship with Nebuchadnezzar—troubles that fill the first half of the Book of Daniel. However, in every difficulty, readers can observe as Nebuchadnezzar grows in his understanding of Daniel's God.

📖 After Daniel interprets a dream for Nebuchadnezzar, what does Nebuchadnezzar do (see Daniel 2:46)? What does the king say?

____

____

____

📖 Compare Nebuchadnezzar's response to a similar response noted in Acts 14:11. What does this tell you about what might happen when ordinary humans display God's supernatural power?

____

____

____

I often wonder where the miracles of the early church era have gone. After all, don't unbelievers still need to see God in action? Why don't we see the miraculous healings and supernatural raising of the dead that were so prevalent in the Book of Acts? Even as I ponder, I remember the inherent dangers of these supernatural displays. So often, when these things happen, those who observe the miracles venerate the humans involved rather than the God whose power supplies the miracles!

Later in Daniel, Nebuchadnezzar observes firsthand the miraculous rescue of Daniel's three friends, Shadrach, Meshach, and Abednego. In Daniel's account, these three men refuse to worship a statue that the king has set up on the plain of Dura. The men are bound and thrown into a blazing furnace. In the midst of the intense fire, the three not only survive, but the king observes a fourth man with the other three men—all of them walking freely among the flames. In the space below, record Nebuchadnezzar's comments as he calls Shadrach, Meshach, and Abednego out of the fire (Daniel 3:28–30). What were Nebuchadnezzar's conclusions about God?

____

____

____

____

At the same time the men of Jerusalem chose disobedience, moving ever closer to the destruction of the city, Nebuchadnezzar is experiencing God through the obedience of his young captives. Knowing that Nebuchadnezzar experienced God in the midst of what Daniel and his friends might have termed their "difficult hour," has your view of your own difficulties changed? Looking at these stories, how do you feel about God's work in men's hearts? Have your thoughts changed as you consider these things? How?

____

____

____

____

____

Daniel's account reminds me of the importance of my faithfulness. As the old saying goes, you never know who is watching. And people do watch. As you walk through life, you'll be carefully observed both by those who know you and those who don't. Your actions influence others as they consider the God you serve.

One more detail. Through Daniel we learn that Nebuchadnezzar has at least one weakness: he is a proud king, willing to take credit for every victory, for every building project, even for the success of his reign. God uses Daniel to warn the king of this weakness. But the king does not respond.

Instead, Nebuchadnezzar endures a seven-year season where he no longer reigns as king. During this season, madness drove him away from the palace, and he took on the characteristics and mannerisms of a wild animal. Only after he acknowledged God's rule was Nebuchadnezzar restored to his kingship. This biblical story is supported by historical documents where Nebuchadnezzar is absent from Babylonian governmental accounts.

According to *The International Standard Bible Encyclopedia,* our sources of extra-biblical information about the life of Nebuchadnezzar come from five hundred contract tablets dated according to the days, months, and years of his forty-three year-long reign. In these records, the encyclopedia clarifies,

> No reference is made in any of these inscriptions to Nebuchadnezzar's insanity. But aside from the fact that we could scarcely expect a man to publish his own calamity, especially madness, it should be noted that according to Langdon we have but three inscriptions of his written in the period from 580 to 561 BC. If his madness lasted for seven years, it may have occurred between 580 and 567 BC, or it may have occurred between the Egyptian campaign of 567 BC and his death in 561 BC.

📖 Read Daniel 4:34–36. When the king's sanity returns to him, what is his response? Do you think this realization changed him permanently? Why or why not?

____

____

____

____

____

BABYLON'S DESTRUCTION FORETOLD

This is what the Lord says—your Redeemer, the Holy One of Israel: "For your sakes I will send an army against Babylon, forcing the Babylonians to flee in those ships they are so proud of. I am the Lord, your Holy One, Israel's Creator and King. I am the Lord, who opened a way through the waters, making a dry path through the sea. I called forth the mighty army of Egypt with all its chariots and horses. I drew them beneath the waves, and they drowned, their lives snuffed out like a smoldering candlewick." But forget all that—it is nothing compared to what I am going to do. For I am about to do something new.

See, I have already begun! Do you not see it? I will make a pathway through the wilderness. I will create rivers in the dry wasteland. The wild animals in the fields will thank me, the jackals and owls, too, for giving them water in the desert. Yes, I will make rivers in the dry wasteland so my chosen people can be refreshed. I have made Israel for myself, and they will someday honor me before the whole world. (Isaiah 43:14–21)

THE REST OF THE STORY

Even as Jeremiah experiences threats and beatings, imprisonment and slander, Daniel tells us that God continues to work on Nebuchadnezzar. Though we'll never know exactly what God had hoped for Nebuchadnezzar and the people of Babylon, I wonder if they might have avoided their destruction. Could repentance have changed the course of Babylon's national history? Might revival have swept the land of the Babylonians, Chaldeans, and Persians? Could Nebuchadnezzar have turned the fate of Babylon? We'll never truly know.

Today, let's go back to Jeremiah and look at his prophecies concerning Babylon. Begin today by reading Jeremiah 50 and 51. In these chapters, the prophet records a lengthy prediction concerning Babylon. To put a date on the prophecy, look at Jeremiah 51:59. When was the prophecy given?

We've already talked about King Zedekiah's trip to Babylon, which happened during the fourth year of his reign. Though we don't know exactly why he made the trip, historians believe that it proves his desire to fall in line with Babylonian authority. Jeremiah gave the message about Babylon's defeat to King Zedekiah via his staff officers. The message was to be read aloud by Seraiah in Babylon years before that nation fell (Jeremiah 51:61). Why do you think that God wanted the captives to be aware of Babylon's coming destruction?

Now that you know when the prophecy was given and the date Nebuchadnezzar took Jerusalem in Jeremiah 52:6, estimate how many years before the city fell, did Jeremiah give this particular message of Babylon's coming destruction?

Now, knowing that Jerusalem fell in 586 BC and that Babylon fell in 539 BC, calculate how many years *before* Babylon's destruction did Jeremiah predict that Babylon would fall?

I hope you don't feel like this study has become a series of story problems from some long forgotten math class. If you have trouble working out the problem, follow along with me. Zedekiah reigned eleven years. The prophecy concerning Babylon's fall was given during his fourth year—seven years before Jerusalem fell. As for the number of years before Babylon was overcome, if you subtract 539 (the year that Darius the Mede took Babylon, mentioned in Daniel 5:30) from 586 (the year that Jerusalem was destroyed) you come up with forty-seven years. Forty-seven plus seven equals fifty-four. Jeremiah predicted the destruction of Babylon at least fifty-four years before the event occurred. Amazing? I think so!

You might also wonder about Darius. According to the *International Standard Bible Encyclopedia,* Darius is mentioned nowhere other than the Book of Daniel. Some guess that Darius received the governorship of the Chaldeans from Cyrus after the fall of Babylon. If this is the case, Daniel refers to him not as conqueror, but as the administrator who took over after Babylon fell. This would make Darius and Cyrus both leaders at the same time.

📖 This prophecy—of Babylon's destruction—is all the more impressive when you consider that the message was given when Babylon was at the height of her power. Pay attention to the accuracy of Jeremiah's predictions! Looking through the following verses, note the very simple details God gives Jeremiah about the fall of Babylon.

(50:3) Where will Babylon's destruction come from? How severe will the destruction be?

____

____

(50:4) When Babylon falls, what will be the result in the lives of the Jews?

____

____

(50:10) What will happen to Babylon after the attack?

____

____

(50:16b) Who will escape?

____

(50:25–26) What will the destruction look like? What else will be involved? (Note the repeated calling forth of archers, to attack the city of Babylon.)

(50:38) What else will be affected? What reason does God give for this event?

____

____

(51:11) Specifically, who will attack? What reason is given for the attack?

____

____

(51:30) What other destruction can the Babylonians expect? Is the empire defended?

____

____

(51:38) When will this destruction happen?

____

Did You Know?

END OF THE BABYLONIANS

According to the *International Standard Bible Encyclopedia* (www.bible-history.com) records of Cyrus exist in the *Cylinder of Nabonidus*, the *Babylonian Chronicle*, and the *Cylinder of Cyrus*. These historical documents tell us that Cyrus, the Persian, overthrew Babylon in October of 539 BC. Though his overthrow of the city was swift, he did not destroy the city—just as the prophets predicted. Historians believe that about two weeks before Daniel's account of the drunken feast, the Persians had engaged the Babylonians just outside the city gates.

Unable to conquer Cyrus' troops, the Babylonians had retreated behind what they believed to be impenetrable city walls. Safely inside, they feasted, while Cyrus' military commanders managed to divert the Euphrates River and wade through the water, entering the city underneath the city walls. Once inside, the people—who were exhausted by Belshazzar's tyrannical reign—gladly hailed Cyrus as the new king. Belshazzar was defeated without incident and died before dawn. With three major cities under his command, Cyrus no longer used Babylon as a capital city.

The Persian empire (largely a portion of Iran) lasted for another two hundred years. By the time Alexander the Great conquered Persia, the city of Babylon lay waste under desert sand.

Jeremiah 45–52

DAY FOUR

THE DESTRUCTION

Fortunately for us, we have another uniquely detailed description of what happens to Babylon. While it does not show us the attack from outside the city, it does explore the event from the most privileged of places—the king's palace. To see the defeat in action, turn to Daniel 5.

Nearly fifty years after the final destruction of Jerusalem, Daniel tells us the new Babylonian king is Belshazzar (who ruled with his father, Nabonidus, in Babylon from 556 to 539 BC). Foolishly overconfident, King Belshazzar has given a great feast for a thousand of his nobles when in their drunken stupor they see an enormous hand begin writing on the palace wall. The fearful king calls for his advisors, who cannot explain the event. Eventually, the king summons Daniel, who by this time is an old man—by some estimates nearly eighty years old. (Remember the length of the captivity is measured from the first deportation from Jerusalem, not from the destruction of the city. Daniel was among those first captives.) Daniel chastises the king for his pride and for his refusal to learn Nebuchadnezzar's lesson. After this correction, Daniel interprets the words written on the palace wall.

📖 According to Daniel 5:25–28, what is the message on the wall?

____

____

____

📖 In Daniel 5:30, the end of the kingdom is described. When did it happen? Who died? Who took over the kingdom?

____

____

____

"That very night Belshazzar, the Babylonian king, was killed. And Darius the Mede took over the kingdom at the age of sixty-two."

Daniel 5:30–31

Now looking back at Jeremiah's predictions, how many of the details can you see fulfilled in this single account? Make a brief list here:

____

____

____

History tells us that Cyrus, the Mede, did not destroy the city of Babylon. In fact, Cyrus thought of himself as a great liberator and an advocate for human rights. He had these words inscribed on a clay cylinder in cuneiform, now identified as *The Charter of the Rights of Nations* (discovered in 1879, now kept in the British Museum, London) "I am Cyrus. King of the world. When I entered Babylon. . . . I did not allow anyone to terrorize the land. . . . I kept in view the needs of people and all its sanctuaries to promote their well-being. . . ." For the most part, he left Babylon as he found it, even allowing government officials to continue in their posts. Eventually Cyrus established another capital in the city of Pasargadae in Fars (modern Iran). (http://oznet.net/cyrus/cyframe.htm)

The rest of Daniel's account, found in chapters 7 through 12, relate to prophecies yet to be fulfilled. If you study the book of Revelation, many of Daniel's prophecies make more sense. Daniel, like Jeremiah, gave messages that pertained to the near future (as in Nebuchadnezzar's season of insanity) as well as events in the distant future (even to what we call the "end times"). Some of these prophecies may have more than one fulfillment.

Read Revelation 18:2–3 (included in the sidebar here). If the book of Revelation pertains to things yet to come, how do you explain the destruction of a great city of Babylon, since the city is already gone?

____

____

____

Some biblical scholars think that the Babylon of Revelation may represent a world system or perhaps even a commercial system. Others think it represents a religious system or a political system yet to come into power. If there is a Babylon yet to come, how might that change your interpretation of Jeremiah 50 and 51?

____

____

____

The truth is, no one can answer these questions categorically. I believe the Word to be both inspired by the Holy Spirit and unerring. Since only part of Jeremiah's predictions in these chapters has already come to pass, I think the chapters might reference two events. The first event would be the fall of Babylon as Jeremiah knew it—the capital city of the Babylonian empire. Obviously, this event has already transpired, when the Medes took the city; over time, the city was abandoned and came to ruin.

The second event might refer to the destruction that John (who wrote the Revelation of Jesus Christ) wrote about in Revelation 18. This is a good example of the way prophetic passages may refer both to an imminent event (the city's destruction) and one in the distant future (the destruction of a system we have not yet identified).

It isn't always easy to understand these passages. But I believe we will understand them as they come to pass. Then, as we watch the events unfold, the prophecies will make perfect sense, and they will affirm the magnificent pre-knowledge and work of God in the lives of men.

REVELATION 18:1–3

After all this I saw another angel come down from heaven with great authority, and the earth grew bright with his splendor. He gave a mighty shout:

"Babylon is fallen—that great city is fallen! She has become a home for demons. She is a hideout for every foul spirit, a hideout for every foul vulture and every foul and dreadful animal, For all the nations have fallen because of the wine of her passionate immorality. The kings of the world have committed adultery with her. Because of her desires for extravagant luxury, the merchants of the world have grown rich."

The Return

Jeremiah 45–52

DAY FIVE

In 538 BC, almost immediately after taking control of Babylon, Cyrus issued a decree allowing a limited number of Jews to return and rebuild their Temple in Jerusalem. Construction on this Second Temple began in 536, seventy years after Babylon's first deportation of citizens from Jerusalem.

We read Ezra's account of this declaration in Ezra 1:1–4. According to Ezra, why does Cyrus issue the decree? Who are these returning people? What are the deportees to do once they return?

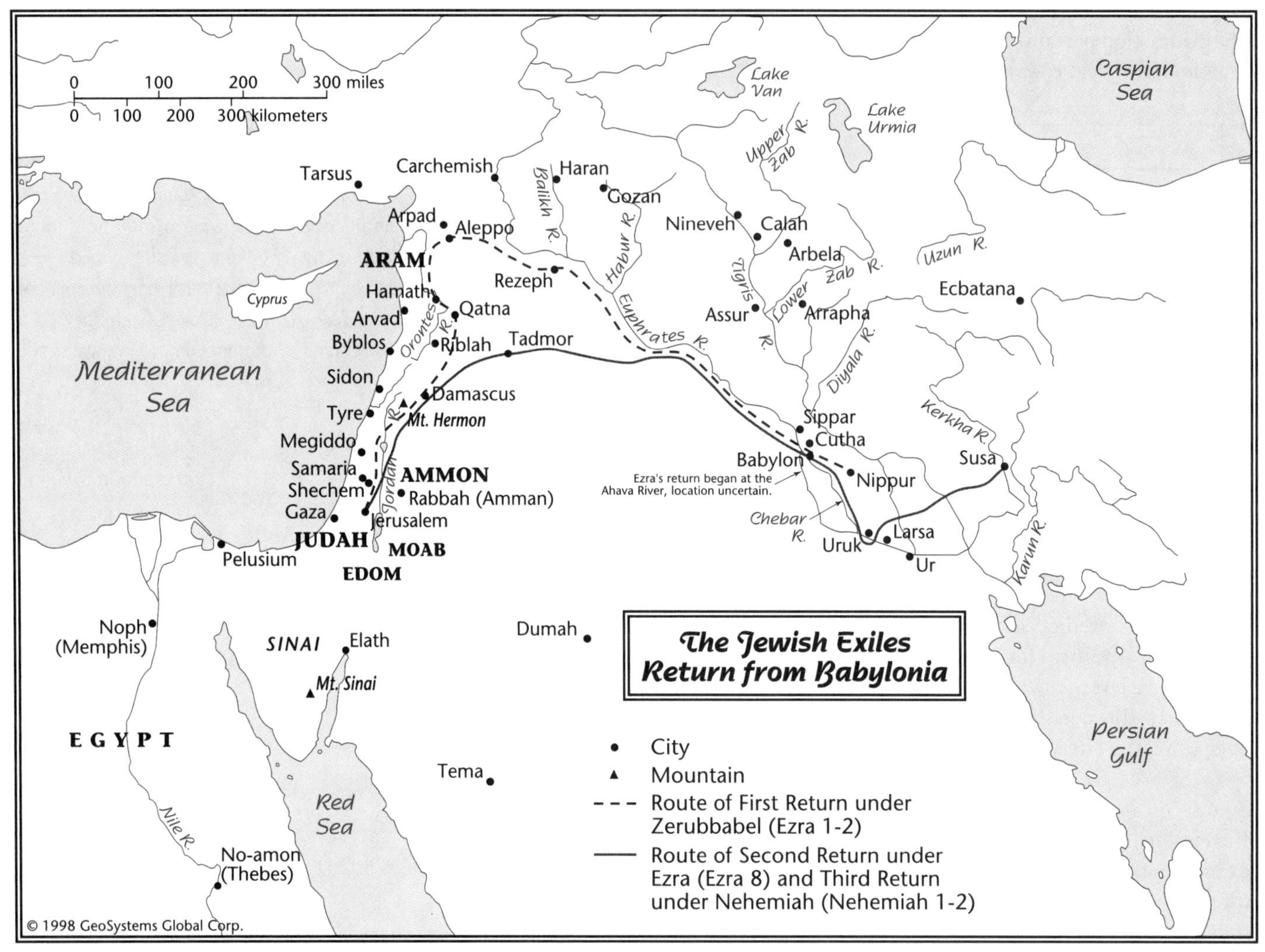

📖 Looking at Ezra 1:7, what else does Cyrus return along with the captives?

Once again, God displays his marvelous power in the affairs of the world and the lives and destiny of non-believers. Imagine a ruler of Persia having conquered the pagan nation of Babylon, choosing to erect a temple for another nation as one of his first priorities!

📖 According to Ezra 2:64, how many people went along in this first wave of returning Jews?

📖 Where did the people settle (Ezra 2:70)?

Remember that while Ezra chronicles this episode, he did not return to Jerusalem until "many years later" (Ezra 7:1). The first of the returning deportees under the leadership of Zerubbabel had one task in mind; they had come back to rebuild the Temple. They started with fervor in 536 BC, laying the foundation of the Temple. But when their enemies heard that they were building, these same enemies sent a letter to the king of Persia, eager to convince him that the building of the Temple was an act of Jewish rebellion.

In response, the Persians stopped the building project. Sixteen years later, in 520 BC, the people resumed building. The temple was finished in 515 BC, nearly twenty-one years after construction began—the first sign of normal religious life for those who had returned from exile.

Ezra returned to Jerusalem in approximately 458 BC. He had been appointed by King Artaxerxes of Persia to train the Jews in their faith, teaching them the laws and regulations of God. He and a number of Jews, carrying an enormous free-will offering, made the arduous four-month journey to Jerusalem during the hottest part of the year. On his arrival, Ezra instructed the Jews in the law and corrected their intermarriage with pagan women of the land.

Now let's look at the Book of Nehemiah. Here, the story begins in the twentieth year of King Artaxerxes' reign. This is approximately 444 BC, thirteen years after Ezra, and almost one hundred years after the first exiles had returned to Israel. At this time, though many Jews had already returned to live in their homeland, others, like Nehemiah continued to serve in exile. Though exiles had returned to the city of Jerusalem, they did not always choose to stay there long term. We'll learn why later in this study.

📖 Looking at Nehemiah 1:1–3, where was Nehemiah living? Who came to visit? Where had they come from?

____

____

____

According to the Iran Chamber Society, the fortress at Susa was located in Khuzestan province, in the hottest part of Iran (http://www.iranchamber.com/provinces/15_khuzestan/15_khuzestan.php). This was a favorite winter residence of the Persian kings and continued to be inhabited through many of the dynasties that followed.

📖 What was the essence of Nehemiah's aspiration? You'll find it in his own words in Nehemiah 2:5.

____

____

____

📖 I include this question just for the joy of it! Look at Nehemiah 7:4. How many people were living in Jerusalem at this time? Why do you think there were so few people living in the city?

____

____

📖 How did Nehemiah solve this low population problem (Nehemiah 11:1–2)?

____

____

CYRUS PROCLAIMS

In the first year of King Cyrus of Persia, the Lord fulfilled the prophecy he had given through Jeremiah. He stirred the heart of Cyrus to put this proclamation in writing and to send it throughout his kingdom:

"This is what King Cyrus of Persia says: "The Lord, the God of heaven, has given me all the kingdoms of the earth. He has appointed me to build him a Temple at Jerusalem, which is in Judah. Any of you who are his people may go to Jerusalem in Judah to rebuild this Temple of the Lord, the God of Israel, who lives in Jerusalem. And may your God be with you!" (Ezra 1:1–3)

THE REMNANT RETURNS

I am the one who exposes the false prophets as liars by causing events to happen that are contrary to their predictions. I cause wise people to give bad advice, thus proving them to be fools. But I carry out the predictions of my prophets! When they say Jerusalem will be saved and the towns of Judah will be lived in once again. It will be done! (Isaiah 44:25–26)

I find it delightful when passages of Scripture, written more than one hundred years apart completely support one another. Like Ezra, Nehemiah found few people living in Jerusalem. Of course it's easy to understand why they didn't choose to stay there; the city had no walls, no physical protection!

However, once Nehemiah rebuilt the walls, he felt it was time to repopulate the city. He did so by sacred lots, choosing one in ten of the Jewish citizens living in the Persian Empire to relocate to the city!

In Jeremiah 31:23–25, the prophet predicts this:

> *This is what the Lord of Heaven's Armies, the God of Israel, says: "When I bring them back from captivity, the people of Judah and its towns will again say, 'The Lord bless you, O righteous home, O holy mountain!' Townspeople and farmers and shepherds alike will live together in peace and happiness. For I have given rest to the weary and joy to the sorrowing."*

"As for God, his way is perfect. All the LORD's promises prove true. He is a shield for all who look to him for protection."

2 Samuel 22:31

Using sacred lot, Nehemiah brought farmers, shepherds and townspeople together to live in the city of Jerusalem, under the protection of the newly completed walls.

As for God, his way is perfect.
All the LORD'S promises prove true.
He is a shield for all who look to him for protection.
(2 Samuel 22:31)

As I Follow God:
In an October, 1990 article, *Christianity Today* published the remarkable story of Robertson McQuilken. After more than 22 years at Columbia Bible College and Seminary, McQuilken served as the college president when doctors diagnosed his wife Muriel with Alzheimer's Disease. Her gradual descent into mental oblivion took her away from a successful Christian radio ministry, a widespread speaking ministry, and eventually left her unable to counsel the many who came to her for personal direction.

Wanting Robertson McQuilken to continue as president, the Columbia College Board provided a daily companion for Muriel. Over time, as her condition continued to deteriorate, even that option no longer satisfied her. Muriel felt peace only with her husband beside her. When it became clear to Robertson that his wife needed his full-time attention, he faced a difficult choice. Should he sacrifice his ministry to care for his wife? With the college enjoying newfound success, should he leave everything to be with her?

Many well-meaning friends reminded him that such a sacrifice would never change her condition; in her mental state, Muriel would not feel the pain of separation for long. Others advised that it would be wrong for him to abandon his thriving ministry for such a futile pursuit. Many suggested that McQuilken institutionalize his wife.

Robertson McQuilken made the hard choice to leave his administrative position. He wrote in *Christianity Today,* "When the time came, the decision was firm. It took no great calculation. It was a matter of integrity. Had I not promised, 42 years before, 'in sickness and in health . . . till death do us part'?"

In caring for his ailing wife, Robertson chose to keep his marriage promise, a choice rarely observed in our culture. As she grew increasingly ill, Muriel grew unable to express herself. She could no longer speak in sentences, often saying "no" when she meant yes. As her mental condition deteriorated, her choices, behavior, and reasoning became increasingly bizarre.

However, Robertson's willingness to care for her—simply because of his promise—becomes a beautiful illustration for the faithfulness of God.

Unlike humans, God **always** keeps his promises. In this last lesson of Jeremiah, we have seen many, many of God's promises, given through Jeremiah, proven true:

- Jeremiah promised destruction of Jerusalem. It was destroyed in 586 BC.
- Jeremiah promised the burning of the Temple. Nebuchadnezzar burned it in the final destruction of the city.
- Jeremiah promised destruction of Babylon. That nation fell in 539 BC.
- Jeremiah promised that the Persians would destroy Babylon while the Babylonians were under the influence of strong drink. He promised the city's water supply would dry up. After blocking the river that fed the city water, Persian troops climbed through the riverbed and took the city while the Babylonian king drank with his friends at a great feast.
- Jeremiah promised that Cyrus would send the Jews home. He did, issuing his first decree only months after the Persians conquered Babylon.
- Jeremiah promised that the city of Jerusalem would be rebuilt. Both the Temple (by Ezra) and the City (by Nehemiah) were rebuilt by returning refugees.

God keeps His promises.

My point is very simple. If God gives His word—whether of good or of evil—you can count on Him keeping it. Through thousands of years and hundreds of pages of Bible history, God's promises have proven true over and over and over again. Those promises given to individuals, those given to nations, those that point to the birth of Jesus, and those given to the Church, all have proven true.

Unlike men, God keeps His Word. You can count on it. Those promises not yet fulfilled—will be!

While we don't always understand His ways, God is consistent in His dealings with people. God's discipline is never random or unexpected. If you need correction, you can be certain that He will make it clear. If you respond, He is merciful. If you rebel, He will continue to correct.

God uses people. He designs us for the task He has in mind. Then, at some point in our life, He calls us to the task. When we respond to His calling, He promises both His presence and the resources we need to carry out our task. God called Jeremiah, and then over the course of forty-six years in ministry—six of those in Egypt—He gave Jeremiah everything he needed to obey. God was with Jeremiah, all through his ministry.

God will use you. He will be with you. He will give you everything you need to accomplish the task for which He designed you. That's pretty exciting news, isn't it?

"So a total of 42,360 people returned to Judah, in addition to 7,337 servants and 245 singers, both men and women. They took with them 736 horses, 245 mules, 435 camels, and 6,720 donkeys."

Ezra 2:64–67

Also recorded word for word in Nehemiah 7:66–69

Notes

Conclusion

Recalling the Lessons of Jeremiah

Every time I explore the Book of Jeremiah I am blessed. Though serving God is never easy, Jeremiah's committed life encourages me to serve God with my whole heart. His life reminds me of how hard it is to remain true when everyone around you chooses falsehood. Because all humans are basically— well *human*— Jeremiah reminds me that every minister faces a tough audience. And yet, like Jeremiah, as I minister I find that God is always faithful:

Every time I explore the Book of Jeremiah, I am blessed.

When I am weak, he makes me strong. When I am discouraged, he gives me words of encouragement. When I don't understand, God finds practical ways to show me his eternal truths. When he calls me to serve him, he gives me everything I need to obey. And when I obey, I discover that God himself works both in and through me.

I am changed when I choose to serve God.

Jeremiah was changed. When God called Jeremiah, he was nothing more than a boy. He had no experience, no resume that qualified him to speak for God. When confronted with God's assignment, Jeremiah focused on his own inability, rather than on God's unending resources. And yet, God chose Jeremiah as His spokesman.

When he began his ministry, Jeremiah struggled with fear. What if the priests and prophets rejected him? How would the people respond? Yet, by the end of the book, this prophet courageously confronts kings and priests, prophets and rebels—exactly as God had told him he would. And in the process of these confrontations, God makes Jeremiah impenetrable, exactly as He promised in Jeremiah chapter 1.

Jeremiah has learned Isaiah's eternal truth. *"Do not fear anything except the LORD Almighty. He alone is the Holy One. If you fear him, you need fear nothing else. He will keep you safe."*

By the end of the book, Jeremiah knew God's abiding presence. Do you remember the many promises God gave Jeremiah in chapter 15?

I will make you secure.
They will not conquer you.
I will protect and deliver you.
I will rescue you.

God kept these promises to his prophet. Jeremiah was secure. Though the people longed to kill him, they could not. Jeremiah lived through the siege to be taken with the captives to Egypt.

He was not conquered. Jeremiah remained true to his ministry. No one convinced him to step down, back away, or to give up.

Jeremiah was protected. He was kept safely in jail, where he had food while everyone else in the city starved.

He was rescued, once by Ebed-melech, (who pulled him from the cistern) and another time by Nebuzaradan (who found him among those chained for the walk to Babylon).

And perhaps the most important promise of all? "I will be with you."

After forty years of ministry, Jeremiah knew the truth of that statement. Jeremiah **knew** God's abiding protection, provision, and presence—not in an intellectual way. Jeremiah experienced God's presence in a very real, very personal way.

Because of his ministry, Jeremiah knew God in a way few other humans ever will.

Because of his ministry, Jeremiah knew God in a way few other humans ever will.

By serving in ministry Jeremiah learned to care for his own people, and to intercede faithfully for them. Jeremiah goes from uninvolved observer, in chapter 1, to deeply concerned priest, longing for his people to know the joy of obedience. When he begins to speak for God, Jeremiah is an accuser. By the end of the book, Jeremiah has become a confessor.

During the course of his lifetime of ministry, Jeremiah comes to a deeper understanding of the human heart. He learns that education and wealth won't protect people from disobedience. He learns that a stubborn and rebellious heart leads to a wickedness so entrenched that it hardens God's people, making even divine correction ineffective.

Idolatry, Jeremiah learns, hurts the idolater most of all.

By the time Jerusalem fell, Jeremiah had served in prophetic ministry for more than forty years. By most contemporary standards, his ministry was an utter failure. Judah's leadership—her kings, priests and prophets—rejected Jeremiah's message. They ignored his warnings. They mocked and ridiculed him. They put him in jail and tried to murder him. Even the common people joined in contempt.

With smoke drifting up from the ashes, and Jerusalem's finest buildings and the city wall nothing more than rubble, most of us would give up. We'd want to cash in our 401Ks and buy condos in Joppa, where we could lie in the sun and forget it all. We might spend the rest of our days nursing our wounded egos and resenting God for calling us to a ministry He knew would never make any real difference.

But Jeremiah did not retire. Even when no one would listen to him, when he found himself taken against his will to Egypt, Jeremiah continued to faithfully minister for God. He interceded for people he knew would not obey. He gave messages to people he knew would never listen. He continued to prophecy about events and disasters he was powerless to change.

Jeremiah did not retire. Even when no one would listen to him, when he found himself taken against his will to Egypt, Jeremiah continued to faithfully minister for God.

But instead of wallowing in the lack of results, Jeremiah continued to faithfully do what he had been called to do.

And because he was faithful, we have the encouraging and truthful account that we have been studying over these many weeks. Jeremiah did not know that he was writing part of the Bible. He had no way of knowing that his words—the words God gave him, along with the account of his ministry—would become part of the unerring and undying testimony of God. He had no way of knowing that those words would live for nearly three thousand years.

He had no idea how influential his life would become. He didn't know that you and I would find a pattern for ministry in his life. Like us, Jeremiah couldn't see the future. He only knew today. Yet, refusing to give up, he served. With no hope of influence, he served. With no hope for change, he served.

That encourages me. It reminds me that I have a limited viewpoint, a limited understanding of my own influence. What seems like utter failure may not be. God may use my work, my words, my actions, in ways that I will never see.

In fact, Jeremiah reminds me that success may have very little to do with our twenty-first century model. It may be something entirely different.

As I consider this principle—that having an influence may be more important than building an empire—I think of the Bible's "little people." The unheroes.

I think of Barnabas, who walked hundreds of miles out of his way to convince Paul to take a pastorate in Antioch (see Acts chapter 11). In Paul, Barnabas recognized something, some divine potential that others had overlooked. Barnabas sensed that Paul would bring some critical blessing to the Antioch church. Because of Barnabas, Paul began a ministry that ended with reaching the known world with the Gospel.

I think of Apollos. While he was an educated man, well-spoken, passionate, and convincing, Apollos had not yet heard of Jesus. In Acts 18, we learn that Priscilla and Aquila saw this young preacher's potential, drew him aside and gave him the very thing his ministry was lacking. By helping him to grow, Priscilla and Aquila had significant influence in the kingdom. Apollos went on to boldly refute the Jews in public debates. His words are quoted in Acts 18:28: *"The Messiah you are looking for is Jesus."*

I think of Paul's nephew, who ignoring his own safety and reputation, took the risk of going to the Romans with news of an assassination plot against Paul. Because of this young boy's courage, Paul's life was spared, and he was taken to Rome where he penned most of the New Testament.

The Bible is filled with men and women who are rarely remembered. They have not become the topic of inspirational speeches. Some are not even named. But these faithful ones had the courage to do the hard thing, the right thing. And because of their actions, they changed the course of history.

Like Jeremiah these faithful servants learned that success may be nothing more than doing what you are called to do, faithfully, to the best of your ability, no matter who is watching, no matter what seems to be the outcome. Success may be nothing more than obeying God and leaving the rest to him.

Jeremiah understood this essential principle. It seems to me that he lived it. That is the way I want to live as well; like Jeremiah, I don't want results to sway me from obeying the God that I love.

Over the years, God focused Jeremiah's call. Like a magnifying glass focuses and concentrates sunlight, obedience focused and concentrated Jeremiah's ministry. Jeremiah willingly obeys God's restrictions. He sacrifices family joy and social connections. He endures rumors and false accusations. As his persecution increases, Jeremiah grows more passionate about God. As he comes to understand God's ways, Jeremiah longs to share his knowledge with people.

Jeremiah discovers that people who know God live what they know.

Jeremiah discovers that people who know God live what they know. They love justice. They spread mercy. They care for the poor and the needy. They defend those who cannot defend themselves.

And Jeremiah learns that genuine repentance can be seen. It is not some secret change of the heart. Rather, genuine repentance is revealed by changed behaviors, in compassion, service, fairness, justice and devotion to God.

As I watch Jeremiah learn about God, I learn as well.

As ironic as it might be, I've chosen 2 Samuel 22:31 as a capstone verse for the book of Jeremiah. In these few simple words, David has captured the overarching message of Jeremiah's book: God's ways are perfect. His words prove true. He protects those who seek refuge in him.

> *As for God, his way is perfect.*
> *All the LORD'S promises prove true.*
> *He is a shield for all who look to him for protection.*
> (2 Samuel 22:31)

We've learned that Jeremiah's God is not just an Old Testament God. This God, who longs to rescue His people from sin, is the same God who sent His only Son, so that everyone who believes in Him will not perish but have eternal life. Jeremiah's God loved Judah so much that He sent prophet after prophet. God gave these prophets to His people, so that they, through repentance, could avoid the punishment their sin demanded. Jeremiah's God is one who does not want anyone to suffer the wages of sin.

Jeremiah's God is a faithful God. When Jeremiah faced punishment, or imprisonment, God provided a way *through* the difficulty—whether it came via a faithful advocate, or a risk-taking rescuer. When men choose to stand alone on the side of righteousness, God does not forget them. Both Baruch and Ebed-melech demonstrate God's faithful provision for those who stand alone against evil.

God longs for His people to choose righteousness. He longs for us to give Him first place in our lives. He longs to be our only source, our own deep well of refreshing truth. He wants to be our first response in the face of trouble.
This is the God that Jeremiah comes to know so intimately.

I hope that you have begun to see God as He is. Jeremiah's God is a God worth knowing. He is a God worth following. He is worthy of everything you are, of everything you have, and everything you will ever become.

He cares for you.

Notes

The Kingdoms of Israel and Judah
0 10 20 30 40 miles
0 10 20 30 40 kilometers
Beirut
Sidon
Tyre
Acco
PHOENICIA
Litani R.
Abana R.
Damascus
Mt. Hermon
Pharpar R.
ARAM
Dan
Kedesh
Hazor
J. Jarmuk
Sea of Galilee
Mt. Carmel
Mt. Tabor
Kishon R.
Ashtaroth
Yarmuk R.
Edrei
Mediterranean Sea
Megiddo
Mt. Moreh
Taanach
Beth-shan
Ramoth-gilead
Ibleam
Mt. Gilboa
Jabesh-gilead?
Jordan R.
Tirzah
Samaria
Mt. Ebal
Succoth?
Penuel?
Mahanaim?
Yarkon R.
Mt. Gerizim
Schechem
Jabbok R.
Aphek
Joppa
Shiloh
ISRAEL
Rabbah (Amman)
AMMON
Bethel
Gezer
Jericho
Ashdod
Aijalon
Jerusalem
Mt. Nebo
Heshbon
Medeba
Bethlehem
Ashkelon
Gath
Mareshah
Hebron
Dibon
Gaza
Dead Sea
Arnon R.
Gerar
Besor Br.
JUDAH
Raphia
Beersheba
MOAB
Kir-hareseth
PHILISTIA
Zered Br.
W. el-Arish
WILDERNESS
Region periodically contested by Judah and Edom
Bozrah
EDOM
Kadesh-barnea
WILDERNESS
© 1999 MapQuest.com, Inc

The Last Kings of Judah

JOSIAH	JEHOAHAZ	JEHOIAKIM	JEHOIAKIN	ZEDEKIAH
Began his reign at age 8, reigned 31 years in Jerusalem. "Never before had there been a king like Josiah, who turned to the Lord with all his heart and soul. . . . And there has never been a king like him since." (2 Kings 23:25) King Josiah went out to fight the Egyptians and was killed in battle. His body was returned to Jerusalem where he was buried. His son, Jehoahaz, became king. (see 2 Kings 22) His revival may have influenced Daniel into becoming a faithful servant of God. Jeremiah preached the last 18 years of Josiah's reign. Reigned from 639 BC–608 BC	Jehoahaz was 23 when he became king and reigned only 3 months. Pharaoh Necco of Egypt jailed Jehoahaz to prevent him from reigning. Jehoahaz was taken to Egypt, where he died as a prisoner. Pharaoh installed Eliakim king. Eliakim was one of Josiah's sons and Jehoahaz' brother. Reigned in 608 BC	Jehoiakim (formerly Eliakim)was 25 years old when he became king and reigned 11 years. During his reign, Nebuchadnezzar of Babylon invaded. Jehoiakim surrendured. About the same time that Nebuchadnezzar invaded, Daniel and his three friends went to Babylon as captives. Nebuchadnezzar led Jehoiakim away to Babylon. His son, Jehoiakin became king. Judah paid tribute to Babylon for 3 years. Reigned from 608 BC–597 BC	Jehoiakin was 18 years old when he became king and reigned 3 months and 7 days. Nebuchadzezzar summoned Jehoiakin to Babylon and established his uncle, Zedekiah, to be the next "puppet" king. Eventually, Nebuchadnezzar released Jehoiakin from prison and gave him preferential treatment as he lived out his days in Babylon. Reigned in 597 BC	Zedekiah (originally named Mattaniah) was another son of Josiah and was 21 years old when he became king and reigned in Jerusalem for 11 years. Zedekiah rebelled against the Babylonians, though he had earlier sworn loyalty to Nebuchadnezzar. 9 years into his reign, Nebuchadnezzar returned to Jerusalem and laid siege to the city. During the fall of the eleventh year of Zedekiah's reign, Nebuchadnezzar broke through the city walls. Zedekiah tried to sneak out of the city by night, but he was apprehended by the invading forces and watched his sons die at Nebuchadnezzar's hands. Then he was blinded, and led away to Babylon. After the city was destroyed, Nebuchadnezzar named Gedaliah as governor. Only months later, Gedaliah was murdered by his own people. The remaining people fled into Egypt, taking Jeremiah with them. (Sources: 2 Kings 25; Jeremiah 40—43) Reigned from 597 BC–596 BC

The Lineage of the Kings of Israel and Judah

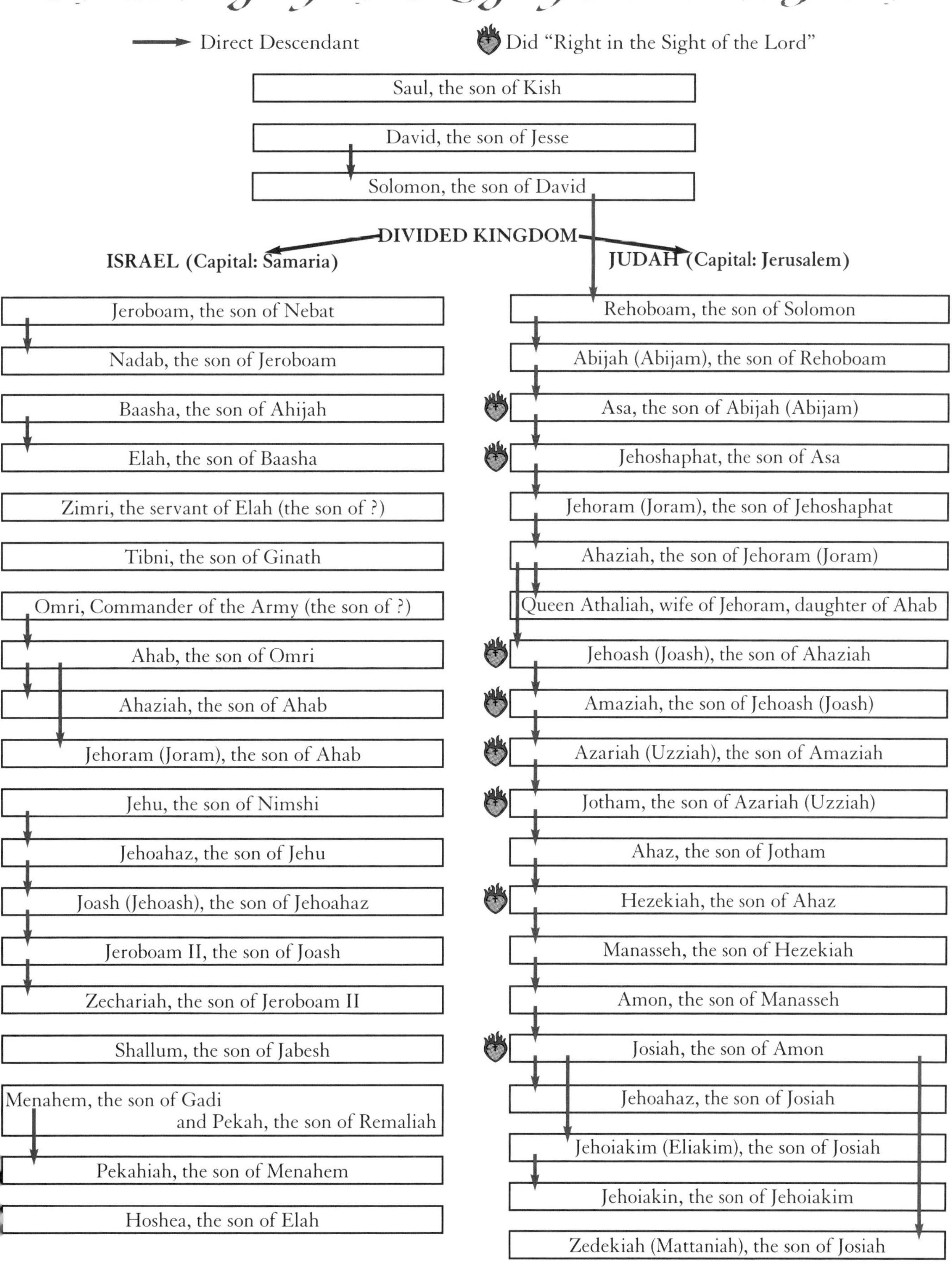

Creation (Origins of God's Family)	Family Develops Through Abraham	God's Family Becomes a Nation	Monarchy Begins with King Saul	Tribal Division under Divided Kingdoms	Submission to Foreign Nations

An Old Testament Timeline

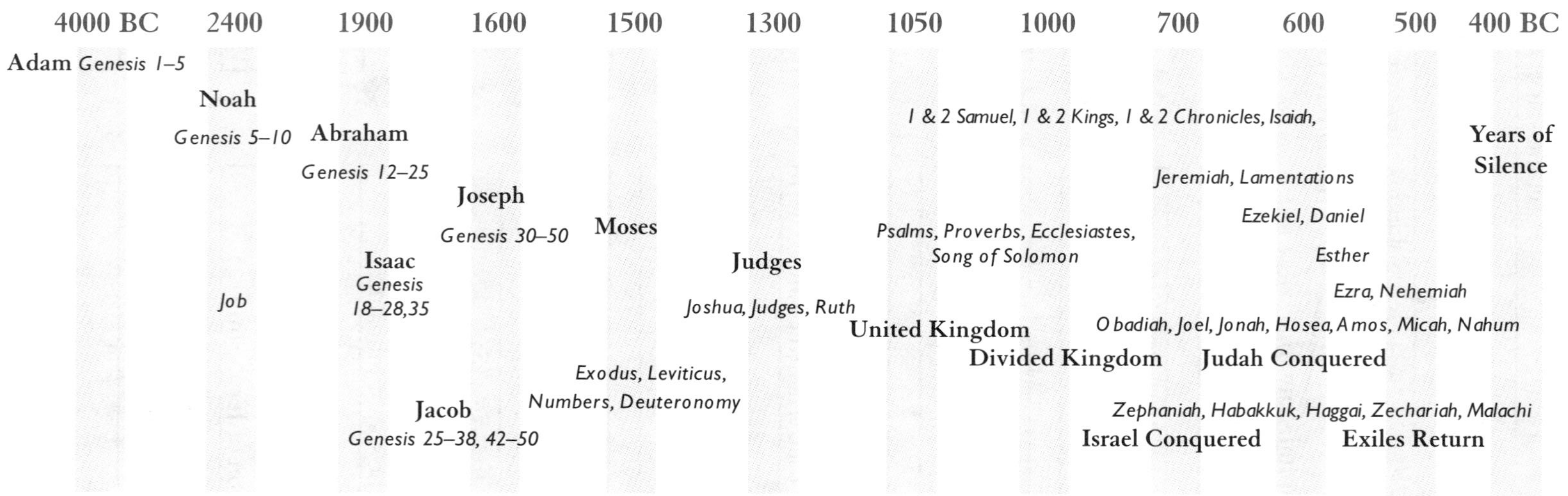

4000 BC · 2400 · 1900 · 1600 · 1500 · 1300 · 1050 · 1000 · 700 · 600 · 500 · 400 BC

Adam *Genesis 1–5*

Noah
Genesis 5–10

Abraham
Genesis 12–25

Joseph
Genesis 30–50

Moses

Isaac
Genesis 18–28,35

Job

Judges
Joshua, Judges, Ruth

Exodus, Leviticus, Numbers, Deuteronomy

Jacob
Genesis 25–38, 42–50

1 & 2 Samuel, 1 & 2 Kings, 1 & 2 Chronicles, Isaiah,

Psalms, Proverbs, Ecclesiastes, Song of Solomon

Jeremiah, Lamentations

Ezekiel, Daniel

Esther

Ezra, Nehemiah

Obadiah, Joel, Jonah, Hosea, Amos, Micah, Nahum

Years of Silence

United Kingdom

Divided Kingdom

Judah Conquered

Zephaniah, Habakkuk, Haggai, Zechariah, Malachi

Israel Conquered

Exiles Return

Timeline of the Kings

United Kingdom — Southern Kingdom (Judah) — Northern Kingdom (Israel)

The names in purple are kings in Israel or Judah. The names in all caps are PROPHETS.

1050 | 1000 | 950 | 900 | 850

SAMUEL
Judge and Prophet
GAD
NATHAN

Saul
1051–1011
David
1011–971
Solomon
971–931

Ishbosheth ruled over Israel
1011–1004
960—Temple finished

David ruled over Judah from Hebron
1011–1004

David ruled over all Israel and Judah from Jerusalem
1004–971

SHEMAIAH IDDO Hanani the Seer OBADIAH JOEL
ODED
Jahaziel the Levite
AZARIAH

Rehoboam
931–913
Asa
911–870
Abijam
913–911
Jehoshaphat
873–848
Jehoram
(Joram)
853–841
Ahaziah
841
Athaliah
841–835
Joash
835–796

Jeroboam I
931–910
Nadab
910–909
Baasha
909–886
Elah
886–885
Zimri
885
Tibni
885–880
Omri
885–874
Ahab
874–853
Ahaziah
853–852
Jehoram
(Joram)
852–841
Jehu
841–814

AHIJAH the Shilonite
"A man of God from Judah"
A prophet from Samaria in Bethel
JEHU, son of Hanani
MICAIAH
ELIJAH
ELISHA

Hiram I of Tyre
981–947
Benhadad I of Syria
900–860
Benhadad II of Syria
860–841

800 | 750 | 700 | 650 | 600

"A Prophet"
(sent to Amaziah)
ISAIAH
MICAH
NAHUM ZEPHANIAH HABAKKUK
HULDAH (a prophetess)
JEREMIAH

Amaziah
796–767
Azariah (Uzziah)
790–739
Jotham
750–735
Ahaz
735–715
Hezekiah
715–686
Manasseh
697–642
Amon
642–640
Josiah
640–609
Jehoahaz
609
Jehoiakim
609–598
Jehoiachin
(Jeconiah)
598–597
Zedekiah
597–586

Jehoahaz
814–798
Joash
(Jehoash)
798–782
Jeroboam II
793–753
Zechariah
753–752
Shallum
752
Pekah
752–732
Menahem
752–742
Pekahiah
742–740
Hoshea
732–722

JONAH
AMOS
HOSEA
ODED

There are no more kings or prophets in the Northern Kingdom.
Foreign peoples are resettled into the land.

605—1st Captivity
DANIEL
Hananiah
Mishael
Azariah
597—2d Captivity
EZEKIEL
Nebuchadnezzar
605–562

Tiglath-pileser I
745–727
Shalmaneser V
727–722
722—Assyria takes Israel into captivity
Sennacherib
705–681
612—Fall of Nineveh

550 | 500 | 450 | 400

HAGGAI
ZECHARIAH
MALACHI

Zerubbabel
536—First Return
536—Rebuilding the Temple
516—Temple completed

Ezra
458—Second Return
Rebuilding the people

Nehemiah
445—Third Return
Rebuilding the walls
and the city of Jerusalem

The Jews are without a king
or a prophet, living under the
dominion of foreign rulers, and
AWAITING THE MESSIAH,
THE TRUE KING OF ISRAEL.

586—Final Captivity
Jerusalem and Temple destroyed

538–Decree of Cyrus to return

Queen Esther

Amel-Marduk
(Evil-Merodach)
562–560
Cyrus
539–530
Darius I
522–486
Xerxes
486–464
Artaxerxes
464–423
Socrates
470–399
Plato
428–348
Aristotle
384–322

Notes

Notes

Notes

Notes

Notes